The

Senior's Guide
to the Internet

Surfing, Shopping, E-Mail and Security

D1004375

Check out these other great titles in the Senior's Guide Series!

The
Senior's Guide
to Digital Photography

The
Senior's Guide
to Dating (Again)

The
Senior's Guide
to Easy Computing

The
Senior's Guide
to eBay®

The

Senior's Guide
to the Internet

Surfing, Shopping, E-Mail and Security

By Rebecca Sharp Colmer,
Certified Senior Advisor (CSA)
and
Todd M. Thomas

EKLEKTIKA PRESS
Chelsea, Michigan

Table of Contents

Table of Contents

Table of Contents

Table of Contents

Table of Contents

Table of Contents

Table of Contents

DISCLAIMER

Every effort has been made to make this book as complete as possible and as accurate as possible. However, there may be mistakes both typographical and in content. Therefore, this text should be used as a general guide and not the ultimate source of information.

LIMIT OF LIABILITY/DISCLAIMER OF WARRANTY: THE PUBLISHER AND THE AUTHORS MAKE NO REPRESENTATIONS OR WARRANTIES WITH RESPECT TO THE ACCURACY OR COMPLETENESS OF THE CONTENTS OF THIS WORK AND SPECIFICALLY DISCLAIM ALL WARRANTIES, INCLUDING WITHOUT LIMITATION WARRANTIES OF FITNESS FOR A PARTICULAR PURPOSE. NO WARRANTY MAY BE CREATED OR EXTENDED BY SALES OR PROMOTIONAL MATERIALS. THE ADVICE AND STRATEGIES CONTAINED HEREIN MAY NOT BE SUITABLE FOR EVERY SITUATION. THIS WORK IS SOLD WITH THE UNDERSTANDING THAT THE PUBLISHER IS NOT ENGAGED IN RENDERING LEGAL, ACCOUNTING, OR OTHER PROFESSIONAL SERVICES. IF PROFESSIONAL ASSISTANCE IS REQUIRED, THE SERVICES OF A COMPETENT PROFESSIONAL PERSON SHOULD BE SOUGHT. NEITHER THE PUBLISHER NOR THE AUTHORS SHALL BE LIABLE FOR DAMAGES ARISING HEREFROM. THE FACT THAT AN ORGANIZATION OR WEB SITE IS REFERRED TO IN THIS WORK AS A CITATION AND/OR POTENTIAL SOURCE OF FURTHER INFORMATION DOES NOT MEAN THAT THE AUTHORS OR THE PUBLISHER ENDORSES THE INFORMATION THE ORGANIZATION OR WEB SITE MAY PROVIDE OR RECOMMENDATIONS IT MAY MAKE. FURTHER, READERS SHOULD BE AWARE THAT INTERNET WEB SITES LISTED IN THIS WORK MAY HAVE CHANGED OR DISAPPEARED BETWEEN WHEN IT WAS WRITTEN AND WHEN IT IS READ. NEITHER THE PUBLISHER NOR AUTHORS SHALL BE LIABLE FOR ANY LOSS OF PROFIT OR ANY OTHER COMMERCIAL DAMAGES, INCLUDING BUT NOT LIMITED TO SPECIAL, INCIDENTAL, CONSEQUENTIAL, OR OTHER DAMAGES.

WE WANT TO HEAR FROM YOU!

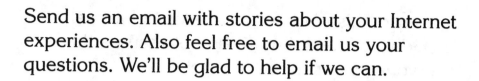

Send us an email with stories about your Internet experiences. Also feel free to email us your questions. We'll be glad to help if we can.

Visit our Web site: <u>www.theseniorsguide.com</u> and send us an email.

You can always contact us the old fashioned way:

The Senior's Guide Series
EKLEKTIKA Press
P. O. Box 157
Chelsea, MI 48118

GETTING THE MOST FROM THIS BOOK

We wrote this book for people of all Internet experience levels, but we do not assume that everyone has used the Internet.

As with any computer-related book, we adopted certain text styles to represent different things:

- Web links are listed with an underline, ex. <u>www.theseniorsguide.com</u>.

- Links within a Web site are shown as underlined words, ex. <u>Home</u>.

- Button labels are written in bold text, ex. **OK**, **Submit**.

- Glossary words use italic text, ex. *HTML*.

The *Internet* is a dynamic place. The information we have provided was accurate at the time of publication. Although the Internet will change, the concepts provided should not.

PART 1

Internet Introduction

Did you know the Internet is the largest computer network in the world? It consists of over 200 million users in the United States and over 812 million users worldwide. There is no one company or organization that owns or controls the entire Internet.

In this Part we provide an overview of the Internet, which includes its good and bad points. Get ready for a world of information and adventure at your fingertips. You are about to leap into cyberspace!

WHAT IS THE INTERNET?

The Internet is a worldwide network of computers. In a network, computers "talk" to each other electronically and allow you to gather or share information from around the world.

Two types of computers make up the Internet: servers and clients. Servers store data (information, pictures, etc.) and "serve" it upon request, to computers known as clients, which is what your computer is considered.

The Internet connects millions of servers and clients together from around the world.

The Internet is often referred to as the Net, the Information Superhighway, Cyberspace, or the World Wide Web (WWW).

In recent years, the use of the Internet for business and entertainment has increased dramatically. Companies and individual users rely heavily on the Internet. Uses include communications, sales, marketing, and entertainment.

HOW DID THE INTERNET ORIGINATE?

The Internet was the invention of the Advanced Research Projects Agency (ARPA and was known then as ARPANet) of the U.S. Department of Defense. It was developed in the late 60's and early 70's as a way for scientists and government officials to communicate and share data.

After its inception, university systems started using it to share research information. Computer scientists, professors and graduate students made the unfriendly interface of the Internet, friendly. They developed the *WWW* and *Web browsers*, more sophisticated *e-mail* clients, and efficient *newsgroup* readers.

Finally, in the early 1990's, the commercial sector became interested in the Internet. For-profit companies have helped evolve it to what it is today.

ARE THE INTERNET AND THE WWW THE SAME?

No, although some may refer to the Internet as the WWW.

The World Wide Web (The Web) links one Web server to another using hypertext links, which are underlined or highlighted words that you click to load a new Web page. Web pages may also have graphics that are hypertext links.

Do not expect every resource or system on the Internet to be accessible through the Web. As a rule, a resource must be coded in *HyperText Markup Language* (HTML) that Web browsers can read. Executable files (.exe's) or data files are examples of resources not easily accessible on the Web.

E-mail and newsgroups are also not part of the WWW. These are separate systems that co-exist with the WWW on the Internet, although some Web sites provide access to these systems.

WHAT CAN I DO ON THE INTERNET?

There are plenty of things you can do on the Internet. For example:

- You can find information on anything from A to Z.

- You can have access to huge databases, libraries and museums all around the world.

- You can send and receive e-mail.

- You can shop online. (www.ebay.com)

- You can find someone to date. (www.seniorsparks.com)

- You can participate in online discussions.

- You can download files such as music and tax forms from a Web site to your PC or Mac.

- You can make money or invest via the Internet.

- You can create your own Web page; a place where people from around the globe can learn about you.

- You can make all of your travel arrangements online for your next vacation or business trip.

HOW MUCH DOES THE INTERNET COST?

Once you are online, most services on the Internet are free. That is, Web sites generally do not charge you to access their site.

To get online, you need to connect to the Internet. ISPs (*Internet Service Providers*) provide connection points to the Internet. ISPs charge for this service.

We provide more details on ISPs and how to choose one in Part 2.

HOW MANY PEOPLE USE THE INTERNET?

This number changes daily. The International Data Corporation estimates worldwide users of the Internet number 812 million.

In the United States it is estimated there are over 200 million users.

It is estimated there are over 27 million Internet users over the age of 65. There is definitely a community of Seniors enjoying the Internet everyday.

IS THE INTERNET SAFE?

The Internet is just like any other media outlet. There are both good and bad information, people and areas. Rest assured, there are more safe sites than unsafe sites.

With care, you may safely shop and invest over the Internet. Millions of financial transactions occur daily without incident. However, you should only conduct financial transactions with reputable, established companies.

Two dangers of the Internet are computer *viruses* and *Spyware*. Without anti-virus software on your computer you run the risk of having your computer hijacked or disabled.

Spyware is a type of virus that allows others to track the Web sites you visit and possibly the keystrokes you type. It can even gain access to personal and financial information on your computer.

With special software it is possible to block access to certain sites which you may find inappropriate whether for yourself or children. Most ISPs can block a lot of the bad stuff at the server level.

See Part 9 for more on Internet security.

WHAT ARE THE BEST PARTS OF THE INTERNET?

The Internet is fantastic. It is the new and future way of information gathering and communication. Here are some of the best features of the Internet:

- Getting information on any topic
- Finding people and businesses
- Financial services and investing
- Paying bills online
- Finding products and services
- Price comparisons and consumer reviews
- Real estate information
- Genealogy searches
- Education
- Buying and selling things
- Travel, maps and city guides
- Digital photography and video
- Marketing and sales
- Games
- Healing and medical information
- Nonprofit organizations
- And more

WHAT IS THE DOWNSIDE OF USING THE INTERNET?

Yes, there are some ugly parts of the Internet. Unfortunately the openness of the Internet also leaves you open to some of the unpleasantries. Here's a list of a few:

- Pornography merchants
- Pedophiles preying on children
- Credit card thieves
- Viruses and spyware
- *Spam* (junk e-mail)

Remember, on the whole, the Internet is a wonderful, mind expanding tool. There is a slight chance that something from the above list will happen to you. However, if you take some basic precautions when using the Internet, you will be able to use the Internet safely.

See Part 9 for more on Internet security.

PART 2

Getting Connected

Getting connected is the first step to using the Internet. Fortunately you have many options ranging from high-speed to low, and high-cost to low.

In this Part we explain how to connect to the Internet. We cover topics ranging from what type of computer to use to the different types of connections that are available.

WHAT DO I NEED TO CONNECT TO THE INTERNET?

You need four things to connect to the Internet:

- A computer or Web appliance (e.g. *WebTV*).
- A *modem*, or other communication device, to connect your computer to an ISP using your telephone line, television cable, *ISDN* line, *DSL* or satellite dish.
- An ISP account to get access to the Internet.
- Browser software to access Internet sites, such as, Microsoft's Internet Explorer, Netscape's Navigator, or Mozilla's Firefox.

There are many ways to connect to an ISP. Figure 2-1 on the next page shows a typical home computer connected to the Internet.

Note that your computer connects to the ISP before connecting to the Internet. This is the case regardless of whether you are a business or a home user. Only a few entities such as universities, ISPs, and government agencies directly access the Internet. Consider yourself very lucky if you have one of these connections.

FIGURE 2-1: CONNECTING TO THE INTERNET

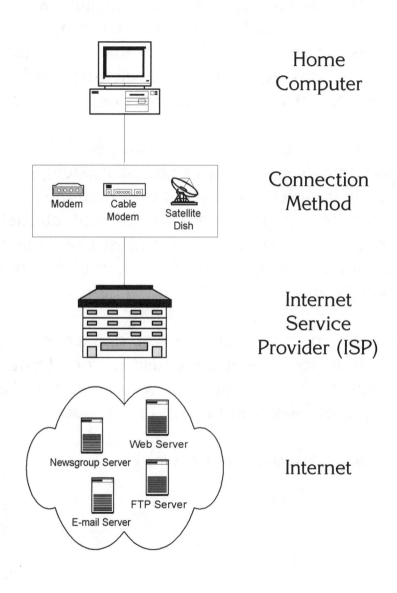

Home Computer

Connection Method

Internet Service Provider (ISP)

Internet

WHAT TYPE OF COMPUTER DO I NEED?

You can use any type of computer, such as a personal computer (PC) or Macintosh, to connect to the Internet. Any brand of PC such as Dell, Compaq, IBM, and Hewlett-Packard will work equally well. Any Mac version works well.

A computer that is less than two years old should have enough power to adequately use the Internet. More important than the computer's speed is the speed of your Internet connection. Computers are almost always faster than the connection speed, so your connection speed is very important.

Some companies produce Web appliances. These devices are built exclusively for Internet access. WebTV is a popular Web appliance that turns your television into a Web browser.

See page 40 for more on WebTV.

HOW DO I GET CONNECTED?

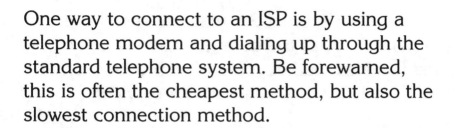

One way to connect to an ISP is by using a telephone modem and dialing up through the standard telephone system. Be forewarned, this is often the cheapest method, but also the slowest connection method.

A better option is a high-speed (a.k.a *broadband*) connection using either a television cable, an ISDN telephone line, an Asymmetric Digital Subscriber Line (ADSL and shortened to DSL for everyday usage) or satellite access.

Broadband connections offer very high connection speeds which will make your Internet experience more enjoyable. The cost differences between dial-up and broadband connections are insignificant compared to the benefits.

Call your local cable TV operator, phone company, or satellite dish provider to find out if broadband is available in your area.

WHAT IS AN ISP?

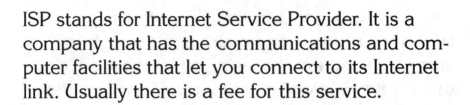

ISP stands for Internet Service Provider. It is a company that has the communications and computer facilities that let you connect to its Internet link. Usually there is a fee for this service.

There are many ISPs from which to choose. The main consideration when choosing an ISP is their available connection speeds.

When considering broadband connections, you may have to use some company other than your local cable television or telephone company. They may not provide a broadband connection in your area.

If you don't mind a slower *dial-up connection* then you can choose an ISP that only offers Internet connectivity using a modem and a telephone line. Make sure that the ISP you are about to choose has a local phone number for you to dial-in to. Otherwise you may be subject to long distance charges for the phone call.

WHY IS CONNECTION SPEED IMPORTANT?

Give careful consideration to the connection speed you decide to use for connecting to the Internet. As a rule of thumb, faster connections create more enjoyable Internet experiences.

Faster speeds also translates into saving time. With a fast connection you can quickly download files, Web pages, and e-mails.

For example, with a dial-up connection it could take five minutes or more to receive an e-mail with pictures of your grandchildren. With a broadband connection it takes a matter of seconds.

You want to use the Internet productively, not spend your time waiting for things to down-load to your computer.

Table 2-1 on the next page compares the speed of the most popular connection methods.

Table 2-1: Internet Connection Speeds

Connection Type	Speed (Kbps)	Comment
Dial-up	28.8 to 56 **Fair**	requires a modem and standard telephone line
ISDN	64 to 128 **OK**	requires an ISDN modem and an ISDN telephone line
Asynchronous Digital Subscriber Line (DSL)	512 to 1,500 **Best**	requires a special modem and standard telephone line
Cable Modem	512 to 1,500 **Best**	requires a cable modem and cable service
Satellite	400 **Better**	requires a special modem and outside antenna

WHAT IS A DIAL-UP CONNECTION?

A dial-up connection refers to connecting your computer to an ISP using a standard telephone line.

It is really just like a phone call, except that the parties are computers rather than people.

Because dial-up access uses normal telephone lines, the quality of the connection is not always good and data rates are limited because of the technology.

The maximum data transfer rates with dial-up is 56 Kbps (56,000 bits per second).

Another negative of a dial-up connection is that your phone line is unavailable while you are on the Internet. Therefore, you cannot make or receive calls when connected. In addition, if you have call-waiting, incoming calls may terminate your Internet connection.

To get around this limitation some people pur-chase a separate phone line just for Internet con-nectivity. This adds additional costs that can equal, or surpass, the cost of a broadband connection.

WHAT IS A BROADBAND CONNECTION?

Historically, broadband has been a type of data transmission in which a single line can simultaneously carry several forms of data at once (e.g. voice and Internet). Cable TV, for example uses broadband transmission to carry television data and Internet communications.

In the Internet era, broadband refers to any Internet connection other than telephone dial-up. Today this definition includes:

- (ISDN) Integrated Services Digital Network
- DSL
- *Cable modems*
- Satellite connections

Another important feature of a broadband connection is that you are essentially always connected to the Internet. You do not have to purposely dial your ISP as you do with a dial-up connection. You either stay connected or the connection process occurs automatically.

HOW DO I CONNECT WITH ISDN?

ISDN lines are similar to standard telephone lines except that they send digital not analog data. This difference dramatically improves data transfer rates.

To use ISDN you need a special digital phone line, that the telephone company may install. You also need an ISDN modem, as standard modems do not work with ISDN lines.

ISDN connections can be tricky to configure. If you choose this route, your telephone company may provide installation services for a fee.

Overall, an ISDN line provides a fast, hassle-free connection to the Internet at a reasonable rate.

HOW DO I CONNECT WITH DSL?

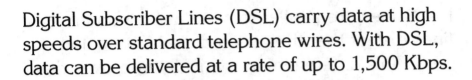

Digital Subscriber Lines (DSL) carry data at high speeds over standard telephone wires. With DSL, data can be delivered at a rate of up to 1,500 Kbps.

DSL users can receive voice and data simultaneously, which means you can talk on the phone while surfing the Internet. You cannot do this with a dial-up connection.

To get DSL, call the telephone company or an ISP that will arrange DSL service. Usually they ship you the equipment needed and you install it yourself. You can also arrange for a technician to install and configure the equipment.

DSL modems connect to a network card (which you may need to add to your computer) or to a USB port. The exact configuration depends upon the modem brand and the provider.

DSL is not available in many rural areas. For DSL to work, you have to live within a couple of miles of your telephone company's central office.

HOW DO I CONNECT WITH A
CABLE CONNCECTION?

Cable access is not available everywhere, yet. If it is available in your area (lucky you), all you have to do is call your cable company.

If you don't already have cable TV wired into your house, they will send someone to install it. The cable company may also provide a cable modem and a network card for your computer. A cable modem usually has a nominal rental fee.

Currently, cable modem access provides the fastest connection to the Internet. You can get some fast download speeds, which means Web pages and e-mail load very quickly.

HOW DO I CONNECT WITH A SATELLITE CONNECTION?

A satellite Internet connection is one in which the outgoing and incoming data are through a satellite. Each subscriber's hardware includes a satellite dish antenna and a transceiver that operates in the microwave portion of the radio spectrum.

Satellite Internet systems are an excellent, although pricey, option for people in rural areas where DSL and cable modem services are not available. The two-way satellite Internet option offers an always-on connection that always surpasses dial-up speeds.

WHAT IS TCP/IP?

When using the Internet you will hear people mention *TCP/IP*. Here's a brief description of it for your reference. (This is nice to know, but you do not need to know it to use the Internet.)

For two computers to communicate, they must speak the same language or protocol. TCP/IP stands for "Transmission Control Protocol/Internet Protocol" and is the language of the Internet.

TCP/IP has two separate parts, TCP and IP. Let's use a postal service letter as an analogy. TCP is the "letter" that contains the data. The latter, IP, is the "envelope" for Internet communications. IP can carry many different types of data. For example, the WWW uses *HTTP* (Hyper-Text Transfer Protocol) and e-mail uses *SMTP* (Simple Mail Transfer Protocol). Both HTTP and SMTP use IP as the envelope.

You need not do anything special to use TCP/IP or any other Internet protocol. All computers and software have it built into them.

WHAT ARE WEBTV AND MSN TV?

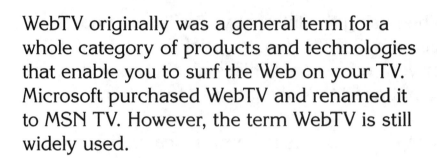

WebTV originally was a general term for a whole category of products and technologies that enable you to surf the Web on your TV. Microsoft purchased WebTV and renamed it to MSN TV. However, the term WebTV is still widely used.

WebTV consists of a small set-top box that connects your television to the Internet. Another term for a WebTV device is an Internet appliance. It has a remote control so that you can navigate the Web from your arm chair or sofa.

The WebTV box accesses the Internet via dial-up or broadband connection and then converts the downloaded Web pages to a format that can be displayed on your TV.

Microsoft charges a fee to use WebTV. You may also have to pay for an Internet connection via an ISP as well.

You can purchase a WebTV Internet appliance at your favorite computer retailer or online at www.Webtv.com.

PART 3

Using the World Wide Web

The WWW is the best known, and most used, part of the Internet. It is very rich in content. You can find almost any information you want in the WWW.

In this Part we will teach you how to find your way around the World Wide Web. You will also familiarize yourself with some of the basic terms associated with browsing. Browsing means to look around the Web.

WHAT IS THE WORLD WIDE WEB?

The World Wide Web (WWW) is a computer network of text, graphical, and *multimedia* information on the Internet. You access the WWW network using software called a Web browser, which displays Web pages, plays music, and downloads files.

A WWW page may be linked to other Web pages using hypertext links that appear as highlighted words or graphics in a passage. Clicking a hypertext link loads another Web page or some other action.

Just to clarify, the WWW is not the Internet. The Internet makes the WWW possible. Other systems such as e-mail and newsgroups also use the Internet.

Using the Web is simple. It's as easy as using the telephone. You don't have to know how a telephone works, you just have to know how to dial.

Try navigating to our Web site and click around. You may find some good stuff. Check out www.theseniorsguide.com.

WHAT IS A WEB BROWSER?

A Web browser allows you to view Web pages and navigate the WWW. You must have a browser if you want to use the WWW. If you have Windows XP, you already have Internet Explorer. Figure 3-1 shows an example of a Web browser with our Web page.

Three of the most popular browsers are: Microsoft Internet Explorer (IE), Netscape Navigator, and Mozilla Firefox.

Although IE dominates with over 90% of people using it, you may want to try Netscape Navigator or Firefox. Both are highly capable and easy to use. If you want to try them you can download them from the Internet.

If your computer doesn't have a browser, you have two choices: purchase browser software at a computer store, or ask your ISP for a Web browser. Ironically, you can't easily download a browser without having a browser.

We focus on IE in this book. Don't despair if you use something different, all browsers use similar concepts. And you can have two different browsers on your computer at the same time.

FIGURE 3-1: WEB PAGE IN WEB BROWSER

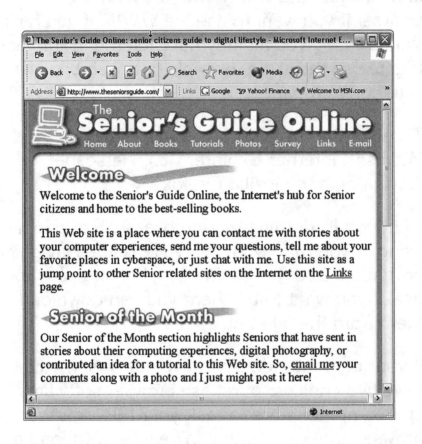

WHAT ARE THE PARTS OF A WEB PAGE?

A Web page can have many parts or elements. Figure 3-2 identifies some common elements you will find on a Web site. Below is a brief description of each:

- Text — The words on a Web page.
- Images — Pictures and graphics augment the text or provide useful information. Images can also be hyperlinks.
- Hyperlinks — Click these to open another Web page. Hyperlinks are the primary method of navigation.
- Menus — Just like Web browsers and word processors have menus, so can a Web page. Menus generally take you to a different area of the same Web site.

FIGURE 3-2: PARTS OF A WEB PAGE

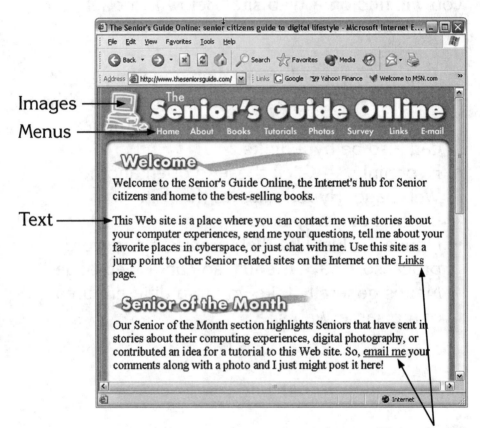

Images —

Menus —

Text —

Hyperlinks

HOW DO I START MY WEB BROWSER?

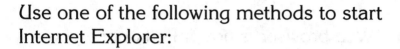

Use one of the following methods to start Internet Explorer:

- Click Start then click Internet (near the top left).
- If you have a browser icon on your Desktop then double-click it.
- Click Start ⇨ Run then type "iexplore" without the quotes.

When your browser opens, it opens to your ISP's default *Home Page* unless you have specified some other Web page.

WHAT SHOULD I KNOW ABOUT A BROWSER?

Using a Web browser is not difficult once you learn the basics. Figure 3-3 on the next page shows some of the more useful parts of Microsoft's IE browser. The following provides a brief explanation of each:

- Arrow Buttons — These move you backward or forward through pages you have already visited.
- Address box — You can type in the *URL* of a Web site to navigate directly to it.
- Home Button — Loads your Home Page. Useful for going back to your start page with a single click.
- History Button — Opens a side bar that shows the most recently visited Web sites. It is handy to return to a Web site that you can't remember the address but remember the content.
- Favorites Button — Opens a side-bar that lists all your favorite Web sites. Useful for easy access to the sites you like the most.

FIGURE 3-3: PARTS OF A WEB BROWSER

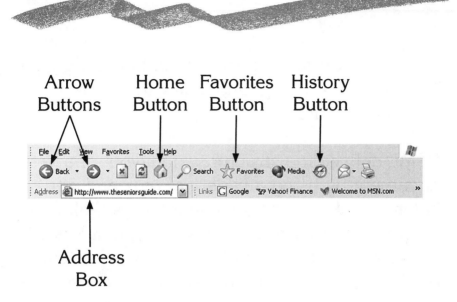

WHAT IS HTML?

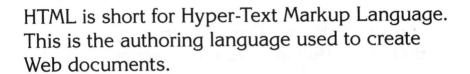

HTML is short for Hyper-Text Markup Language. This is the authoring language used to create Web documents.

HTML defines the structure and layout of a Web document by using a variety of tags and attributes. HTML pages may contain hyperlink connections to other documents. A hyperlink is a connector between the Web page you are currently viewing and another somewhere else. It is a signpost to take you to other Web pages with related information. It can appear as an icon, graphic, or word in a file, that when clicked, automatically opens another file for viewing.

A link is usually underlined or displayed in a different color. If the link happens to be an image, the mouse pointer turns into a "hand" to show that the image is a link.

To follow a link, click on the highlighted text or image. You will jump to the new site.

WHAT IS YOUR HOME PAGE?

As we mentioned, your Home Page is the first page loaded when you start your Web browser.

If you use Internet Explorer, the Home Page is automatically set to MSN, which is the Microsoft Network. This page summarizes a little bit of everything — weather, news, financial, etc.

If your ISP provided the browser, chances are that the ISP's Website is the default Home Page.

Once you get comfortable with the Web, choose your own Home Page so you can access the information you use the most. Some people set it to their investment broker's site so they can easily track their investments. Others are more interested in news or weather.

Or you can keep MSN as your ISP's Home Page.

HOW DO I NAVIGATE THE WWW?

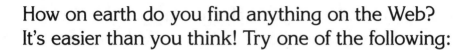

How on earth do you find anything on the Web? It's easier than you think! Try one of the following:

- Type the URL into the address box and press ENTER.

- Use a search tool/*search engine* to generate a list of Web sites with content on a certain subject.

- Refer to Web directories, which are similar to the Yellow Pages.

WHAT IS A URL?

URL stands for Uniform Resource Locator. It is the standard way of referencing a Web site or other Web resource. It is analogous to the address on a letter.

The following are examples of URLs:

- http://www.theseniorsguide.com
- http://www.google.com
- http://www.meetasenior.com
- http://www.seniorsparks.com

Most companies such as Coke, Ford, Land's End, and Sears use their corporate name as their URL. For example:

- http://www.coke.com
- http://www.landsend.com

One note, with most browsers, you do not have to type http://. The browser recognizes what you are trying to do if you just type the Web address starting with the www.

WHAT ARE THE PARTS OF A URL?

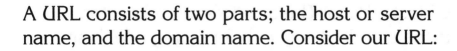

A URL consists of two parts; the host or server name, and the domain name. Consider our URL:

www.theseniorsguide.com

"www" is the hostname, which is the name of the Web server. The hostname can be anything, such as "mail", "news", or "images."

The "theseniorsguide.com" is our domain name, which is unique on the Internet.

Combining the hostname and domain name creates a unique address so you can navigate to it. It's like your street address, P.O. Box, or telephone number.

WHAT IS A .COM, .EDU, .NET, .GOV, .ORG?

The last part of a URL name signifies the type of entity the domain is. Consider our URL: www.theseniorsguide.com. It is a .com, which is a commercial type of domain.

There exist several different suffixes you will find as a URL. Here's a list of the most common and what type of entity they represent:

- .com — commercial bodies
- .edu — educational institutions
- .gov — U. S. government
- .mil — U. S. armed services
- .net — network operators
- .org — other organizations

Because the Internet is growing rapidly, new domain suffixes were created. They include: .info, .biz, .tv, .us, .cc, .name, .bz, .co. Countries may have their on suffix such as .uk (United Kingdom), .de (Denmark), .nz (New Zealand), and .ch (China).

WHAT IS THE DIFFERENCE BETWEEN
http:// AND https://?

As mentioned, the prefix http stands for HyperText Transfer Protocol and refers to the language used by your browser to access and display Web pages.

The prefix https signifies a secure, or encrypted, version of http. Most online merchants, banks, and brokerages use https as their communication method. This ensures your financial information is encrypted so others cannot read it.

As a user, you need not worry about choosing http or https. Your browser switches between the two as needed.

Nonetheless, when you start shopping or banking on the Internet, just make sure the URL in the address bar starts with https://.

HOW DO I FIND INFORMATION ON THE WWW?

With hundreds of millions of Web pages posted on the Internet, the only efficient way to find information is to perform a keyword search or to reference a WWW directory. Either method is simple and easy to use.

A search lets you specify a topic using keywords (e.g. Medicare) and review a list of relevant sites. You perform searches at Web sites that have search engines. The most popular WWW search site is *Google*, which we cover in more detail a little later.

A WWW directory is like an Internet yellow pages directory. Like search engines, special directory sites exist. You look up a topic and navigate to more specific information using hyperlinks.

Google has a directory, but Yahoo! is the most popular Web directory.

WHAT IS A SEARCH ENGINE?

A search engine is a Web-based program that lets you do keyword searches for Internet content. The search engine is a program you access via a Web page, so you need not install any software on your computer.

Search engines work by indexing Web pages. This is no small task. Companies use auto-mated indexers called robots, or bots for short. These programs "crawl" the Web by follow-ing the hypertext links on each Web page. It indexes each new page it finds and places the information in a database.

Search engines have become fairly sophisticat-ed. Not only is text indexed, but images, videos, and music. You can search for images of the Grand Canyon, videos of George Bush, or music by Count Basie.

In other words, you can search for anything you want, and typically find information on it.

WHAT ARE SOME POPULAR SEARCH ENGINES?

Google is by far the most popular search engine. It has a very simple interface, returns results fast, and has indexed most of the Web. Regardless of what you are looking for, Google will definitely point you in the right direction.

Other search engines exist that perform very well. Some specialize on certain topics while others provide more general information. Here's a short list of some popular search engines:

- www.google.com
- www.search.msn.com
- www.dogpile.com
- www.askjeeves.com

Search engines are typically free. You should never have to pay for an Internet search. If a site asks you for money to perform a search, leave that site immediately.

HOW DO I SEARCH USING GOOGLE?

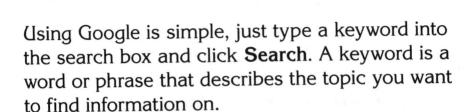

Using Google is simple, just type a keyword into the search box and click **Search**. A keyword is a word or phrase that describes the topic you want to find information on.

Figure 3-4 on the next page shows an example of a Google search for "Peanut Butter."

The more specific the keyword is the better. Broad keywords like "cars" will return a large number of irrelevant results. Narrow keywords like "Cadillac" will return much more specific information. So if you want links related to rose gardening, instead of "flowers" try "roses", or more specifically, "rose gardening."

Remember one thing. A search engine looks for the words you type in the search box, and not necessarily exactly what you are searching for. As an example, you are searching for a choco-late chip cookie recipe. You type "chocolate chip cookie recipe" in the search box and it finds a page with those words on it, but there might not be a recipe.

Figure 3-4: Google Home Page

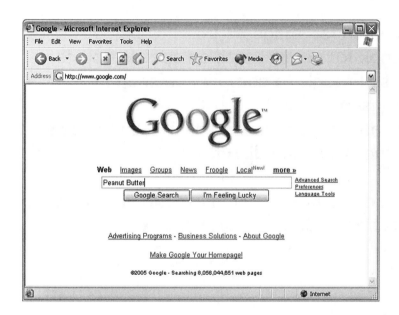

WHAT TYPE OF SEARCHES CAN I DO ON GOOGLE?

Not only does Google let you search for information on Web pages, you can perform many different types of searches. For example, you can:

- Search for images.
- Look for news stories on specific topics.
- Use Froogle to comparison shop for consumer goods.
- Search for conversations in the Groups section.
- Find maps and directions.

You access these specific sections by clicking the links above Google's search box.

WHAT IS THE GOOGLE TOOLBAR?

The Google Toolbar makes searching the Web very easy. It is a toolbar that is displayed in Internet Explorer, just like the Address and Links toolbars. Figure 3-5 shows the Google Toolbar.

Not only does the Google Toolbar allow you to search the Web from any Web site, it provides the following features:

- *Pop-up* ad blocking to reduce or eliminate annoying pop-up windows.
- Search word highlight in Web pages to help you quickly find the information you wanted to know about.
- Automatic form fill-in so you don't have to type your name and address every time you complete a Web form.
- If you do a lot of searching, having the Google toolbar added to Internet Explorer, is a real step saver.

For more information and to download the Google Toolbar, use your browser to go to www.google.com, or more specifically, toolbar.google.com.

FIGURE 3-5: Google Toolbar

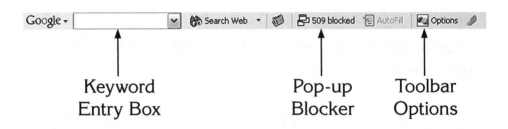

Keyword
Entry Box

Pop-up
Blocker

Toolbar
Options

HOW DO I USE THE GOOGLE TOOLBAR?

The Google Toolbar lets you search the WWW without first going to Google. Just type your keywords in its address bar and press **Enter** or click the **Search Web** button. A Google Web page appears with your search results.

Next click a link of interest in the results to view the Web page. For fun click the **Highlight Keywords** button to see all your keywords on the search page.

CAN I SAVE MY FAVORITE WEB SITES?

Yes. You can save the URLs of your favorite Web sites so you don't have to retype them every time. Internet Explorer calls it adding to your "Favorites". Netscape calls it adding to your "Bookmarks".

When you find a site that you like and want to save the URL:

1. Click the **Favorites** menu to open the dialog box shown in Figure 3-6 on the next page.
2. Enter the name of the page you want to save. The name will usually default to the Web page name.
3. If you want to categorize the Web site, click the **CREATE IN** button. Figure 3-7 on the next page is the dialog box showing the Folders window. Either choose an existing folder or click **New Folder** to add one.
4. Click **Add to Favorites** to add the Web site to your Favorites List.

FIGURE 3-6: ADD TO FAVORITES DIALOG BOX

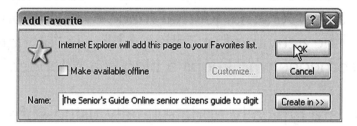

FIGURE 3-7: FAVORITES CREATED IN DIALOG BOX

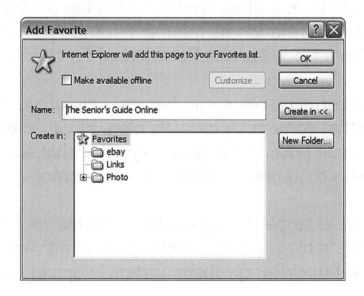

WHAT IS A BLOG?

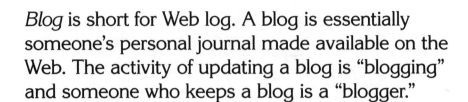

Blog is short for Web log. A blog is essentially someone's personal journal made available on the Web. The activity of updating a blog is "blogging" and someone who keeps a blog is a "blogger."

Blogs are typically updated daily using software that allows people with little or no technical background to update and maintain the blog. Postings on a blog are almost always arranged in chronological order with the most recent additions featured most prominently.

Blogs exist on every topic imaginable. Some operate in real-time, which means the blogger enters information as it happens, such as during the Super Bowl or the Presidential Elections.

Used correctly blogs can be very helpful. Just be sure that you read a credible blog. Because anybody can post a blog, you might find that some are less than honest and have ulterior motives.

For an example of a good blog, check out Flip Colmer's blog about searching for World War 2 MIAs: http://Bentpropsupporters.blogspot.com.

WHAT IS UPLOADING AND DOWNLOADING?

If you send a file to another computer, you upload a file. If you receive a file from another computer, you download it.

The WWW allows both. You can easily download a file from a server using a Web browser. Unfortunately browsers can't readily upload a file to a Web server.

To upload files without a browser you typically use a *File Transfer Protocol* (FTP) and special software called and FTP client.

Most people never upload files to a server, so you don't have to worry about this. Whew!

HOW DO I DOWNLOAD A FILE
FROM THE WEB?

When you download a file, you are retrieving data from an online service and storing it on your own computer.

Downloading a file means the Web server sends you a copy of the file. To start a download, click on the link and follow the prompts.

Usually a "Save As" dialog opens to ask you where on your hard drive you want to save the file. Remember where you save the file! Click the **Save** button and the file download begins.

Figure 3-8 on the next page shows the File Download dialog box after it completes. After it finishes you can click the **Open** button to view it immediately or the **Close** button to look at it later.

Always look at how big the file is before downloading it. You need to make sure that you have enough space on your computer to hold it. Also, take into consideration how much time it will take to transfer. This is another reason a broadband connection is nice to have: large files download rapidly.

Figure 3-8: Internet Explorer Download Dialog Box

WHAT IS FTP?

As we mentioned, FTP stands for File Transfer Protocol. It is a way to transfer files between computers. Unless you have an specific need for it you probably will never use it. Most servers can transfer files using http. However if you run across a server that uses FTP, your browser will automatically use that protocol.

Nowadays, FTP is usually used to upload files to a Web server. For example, if you have a Web site, you would use FTP to upload the HTML files to the server.

To do so requires an FTP client. Many free versions exist on the Web. Just do a Google search on "free FTP clients" and you will get a long list of sites.

Here's a short list of some popular, easy to use, FTP clients and the sites you can download them from:

- WS_FTP — www.ipswitch.com
- Smart FTP — www. smartftp.com
- FTP Voyager — www.ftpvoyager.com

WHAT IS A POP-UP AD?

Pop-up ads are windows that "magically" appear when you navigate to a Web page. These windows contain advertisements with links to a company's Web site.

Advertisers use pop-ups to aggressively market items for their clients. Creators of pop-ups have gotten very clever. The pop-ups now look like small applications with misleading messages or warning messages.

If you get a pop-up ad, and you eventually will, you can either choose to:

- Close the Window by clicking the "X" in the upper left corner of the Window.
- Follow the links in the pop-up ad if you are interested in the company's services. We don't recommend this method as you never know how trustworthy the pop-up ad is. Your best bet is to do a Google search on the company and follow the resulting links.

HOW CAN I PREVENT POP-UP ADS?

Life on the WWW is a life with pop-up ads. You can't prevent them, but you can lessen them.

Pop-up ads have become so bothersome that a cottage industry flourished around eliminating them. That is, numerous companies make software to combat the problem.

The software is called pop-up blockers. Many options exist from free to pay. Most anti-virus software now has pop-up blockers, usually for a fee though.

Internet Explorer has a pop-up blocker, as does the Google Toolbar. Both run automatically and do a decent job.

If you don't use the Google Toolbar, do a Web search for pop-up blockers to get a large list of options.

Pick a blocker program that allows you to choose which pop-ups to block. Some pop-ups are not ads at all, but may be integral to what you are trying to accomplish at a Web site.

HOW DO I FIND PEOPLE ON
THE INTERNET?

Just like you can search for music, files, news stories, and much more, you can also locate a person's address and phone number.

Nationwide phone books exist that work much like Google. Type in the name, city and state if you know it. You should get back the address and phone number of the person you're looking for. Try searching for your name and see how it works.

Some popular people search sites include:

- people.yahoo.com
- www.switchboard.com
- peoplesearch.lycos.com
- www.whitepages.com

CAN I PRINT A WEB PAGE?

Yes. It's easy. Either:

- Click the **Print** button on the Web browser button bar.

Or

- Click **File** then **Print** on the Web browser's menu.

Be forewarned, printed Web pages may not look like what you see on the screen. Web pages are created to be displayed, not printed.

Some sites may have a link that will display a print-friendly version of a page. As you might expect, these pages look mediocre on screen, but look great in print.

PART 4

Multimedia
Web Content

Now that you have an idea about what the WWW is, you can try to experience some of its most exciting content; audio and video.

This Part introduces the multimedia content of the WWW. We cover what types of media you can view or listen to and how to do it.

WHAT IS MULTIMEDIA?

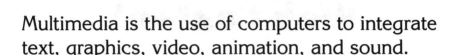

Multimedia is the use of computers to integrate text, graphics, video, animation, and sound.

Web sites use multimedia to create appealing and catchy content to keep you interested in their site.

Some Web sites not only use multimedia in their Web pages, they provide multimedia content. Some focus on song files, while others stream sound and video. You can even watch live events via Web cams!

To best experience the multimedia WWW you need to have a broadband Internet connection. Dial-up modems do not provide the speed necessary to download large media files or adequately listen to streaming music.

WHAT ARE JAVA, JAVA APPLETS, AND JAVA SCRIPT?

Sun Microsystems developed Java as a programming language to enhance Web sites and Web pages. However, Java has grown into a full feature programming language used in as many non-Internet applications as Internet.

Small Java applications built for Web pages are called applets. Most Web browsers can run applets without any problem.

JavaScript is a Web page script language from Netscape. It works in tandem with HTML. JavaScript is used in Web site development to do such things as:

- Automatically format dates on a Web page.
- Cause a linked-to page to appear in a pop-up window.
- Create dynamic drop-down menus on Web pages.
- Cause text or a graphic images to change during a mouse rollover.

Don't worry. Most of this works in the background and you don't need to do a thing.

WHAT IS A BROWSER PLUG-IN?

A *plug-in* is an auxiliary program that works inside your browser to provide extra functionality. Because they are auxiliary programs you must download and install plug-ins yourself, which is very simple. In fact, most are self-installing.

Plug-ins allow you to do things in your browser that you normally do on your computer. For instance, Microsoft has a plug-in that allows you to read Microsoft Word files within Internet Explorer or Netscape Navigator. Excel, Adobe and many other popular programs have plug-ins that provide similar functionality.

Because a plug-in integrates within the browser, you must make sure the plug-in is compatible with your browser. Plug-ins created for Internet Explorer will not work with Netscape Navigator or Mozilla Firefox. Plug-ins are also operating system dependent. Mac plug-ins will not work on a PC and vice-versa.

WHAT ARE COMMON BROWSER PLUG-INS?

Many plug-ins exist, here are the most popular:

- Adobe Reader — lets you read PDF files in your browser.
- Java — allows Java applications and applets to run in your browser.
- Windows Media Player — allows you to listen or view content in Windows Media Player format (.wma, .wmv).
- *QuickTime* — allows you to listen or view content in QuickTime format (.mov).
- *RealPlayer* — allows you to listen or view content in RealPlayer format (.rm, .ram).
- Shockwave/Flash — dynamic content players for browsers.

Don't worry about when to download a plug-in. If you need it and don't have it, a dialog box will appear and start the process. After it downloads it will likely install itself. You may have to restart your computer to get the plug-in to work. A dialog box will tell you if you need to restart.

WHAT IS SHOCKWAVE OR FLASH?

Shockwave and Flash are both multimedia programs that allow you to listen to, and see, content that was created in Macromedia's Shockwave and Flash formats. A number of Web sites use these formats and you will not see this content unless you get the appropriate plug-in.

The good news is that almost every Web site that uses Shockwave and/or Flash, offers free, convenient downloads of the viewers.

CAN I LISTEN TO MUSIC ON THE INTERNET?

Yes. There are several different ways to listen to music on the Internet.

The first is streaming audio, which is when a Web site "broadcasts" either recorded or live music over the Internet. A media player on your computer plays the audio "stream" as it arrives.

The second method uses audio files that you download to your computer. Unlike streamed formats, you have to download the file before you can play it. These formats are used for short sound bites, synthesized music and CD-quality recordings.

There is plenty of music and audio content on the Internet. Most radio stations and shows stream their live broadcasts over the Internet.

HOW DO I LISTEN TO INTERNET MUSIC?

Listening to music on the Internet requires a multimedia player such as Windows Media Player, RealPlayer, or QuickTime.

Once you have a media player, listening is simple. Just navigate to a Web site that has either streaming audio or downloadable files.

For fun, listen to classical music at the Seattle, WA based www.king.org. You'll find easy to follow links that point to you the streaming audio.

WHERE CAN I DOWNLOAD A MULTIMEDIA PLAYER?

You can download media players from the company's Web site that makes them. Here is some information on the three, dominant media players:

- Window's Media Player — packaged with Windows. But if for some reason you do not have it, go to <u>www.microsoft.com/mediaplayer</u> to download it.
- RealPlayer — A very popular media player that you must download and install yourself. Go to <u>www.real.com</u> to download either the free or pay version. RealPlayer also plays RealAudio files, which have a .ra or .ram extension.
- QuickTime — The media player that started out on the Macintosh platform but now runs on Windows as well. Go to <u>www.apple.com/quicktime</u> to download the media player.

CAN I WATCH VIDEOS ON THE INTERNET?

Yes, you can also watch video on the WWW. All you need is one of the media players (Windows Media Player, RealPlayer, QuickTime).

Web sites may either stream video content or provide it via files. As you might expect, video files are much larger than audio files and take longer to download. A broadband Internet connection is really needed if you want to download video.

When you start watching videos on the WWW you will likely run into these file formats and their default media player:

- .asf, .wmv, .avi — Windows Media
- .rm, .ram — RealPlayer
- .mov, .qt — QuickTime movies
- mpg, .mpeg — Either Windows Media, RealPlayer, or QuickTime

WHAT ARE MP3 FILES?

The *MP3* file format is the de-facto format for sound files. You can find all types of music in MP3 format; pop, big band, classical, country, jazz and all other types.

People create MP3s by copying them from music CD's they already own. Now recording companies are distributing MP3s online with anti-piracy features.

Many devices, such an Apple's iPod, play MP3 files. You can transfer them from your computer to the iPod or from the iPod onto your computer.

If you are into music, you'll be listening to MP3s a lot.

ARE SHARING MP3 FILES ILLEGAL?

It is not illegal to make MP3's from your own CDs. However, it is illegal to give those MP3's to someone else or download MP3s of copyrighted material off the Web.

Sharing MP3s is like making a copy of a Stephen King book and giving it out. The artist loses all royalties associated with the work. And that is just not right. You're not copying our book are you?

In recent years the recording industry has become very strict on MP3 sharing. Many sites dedicated to MP3 swapping have been shut down.

Some sites sell legal copies of music files. Apple iTunes is by far the most popular. Check www.itunes.com for more information.

WHAT ARE COMMON AUDIO FILE FORMATS?

Just like there are many different types of music, there are many different types of file formats. Some were created by companies hoping that it would become THE standard. As a result you may run across a variety of music formats.

As we mentioned, there are two primary types of audio on the WWW: high-quality sound files and streaming. Here's a list of the file formats associated with each:

The most common high-quality audio include:

- .wav
- .mp3
- .mpeg, mpg
- .rm, .ram

Popular streaming audio formats:

- .ra
- .ram
- .wma

WHAT ARE ACTIVEX CONTROLS?

ActiveX is a technology from Microsoft that enables interactive content for the WWW. With ActiveX controls, Web sites come alive using multimedia effects, interactive displays, and sophisticated applications that create a user experience comparable to that of stand-alone applications.

ActiveX controls are essentially custom plug-ins. Web site developers create these controls to give a browser more functionality.

PART 5

Online Shopping and Auctions

With the Internet, finding a bargain has never been easier. Online shopping and auctions bring the world's selection of goods and services to your doorstep. Online shopping and auctions offer advantages — particularly when you can't find something as cheaply, if at all, in your home town.

In this Part we provide an overview of online shopping and offer tips on how to keep safe while doing it.

WHAT SHOULD I KNOW ABOUT SHOPPING ON THE INTERNET?

Shopping on the Internet is as safe as you make it. As in the brick and mortar world, there are both good and bad sites. Most are reputable. Some may try to scam you while others may practice "bait and switch."

However, following some simple guidelines will help keep you safe. Here's a list of some common-sense tips:

- Shop only at reputable sites.
- Use a credit card so you can dispute a charge if needed.
- Never send credit card or passwords via e-mail.
- Always read the site's return policy.
- Understand an online merchant's shipping policy.
- Ensure the site is using a secure server.
- Check with a rating site on any business site you do not know.

WHERE CAN I SHOP ON THE INTERNET?

Almost all major retail chains have Internet sites where you can buy goods and services. Plus, a plethora of purely Internet-based businesses exist for your shopping pleasure.

Here's a very short list of places to shop:

- Target: www.target.com
- Wal-Mart: www.walmart.com
- Lands End: www.landsend.com
- Amazon: www.amazon.com
- Barnes & Noble: www.bn.com
- Sears: www.sears.com

IS SHOPPING ON THE INTERNET SAFE?

Shopping on the Internet can be a wonderful experience. It is convenient and fun. However, it is very important for online shoppers to take simple steps to protect their personal information.

Follow these tips for making your online shopping experience safer:

- Don't fall victim to *phishing* e-mails. Never click on an unsolicited e-mail. If you are interested in the product or service mentioned in the e-mail, go directly to the Web site instead.
- Use a secure server if you are submitting information to a Web site.
- Be suspicious of any e-mail that asks for your personal financial information.
- Monitor your bank and credit card statements carefully. If you have been scammed, notify your financial institution and/or credit card company immediately.

WHAT IS SECURE SHOPPING?

There are numerous encryption technologies used for secure shopping. These are used to protect your credit card number and personal information while transmitting it from your Web browser to the online store's Web server and payment gateway.

Secure sites use *SSL* (Secure Sockets Layer), a protocol for transmitting private data via the Internet. SSL works by using a private key to encrypt data that is transferred over the SSL connection.

Besides financial transactions, many Web sites use SSL to accept confidential user information, such as credit card and Social Security numbers.

HOW CAN I IDENTIFY A SECURE SERVER?

There are several ways to identify a secure server:

- Secure Web addresses begin with https:// rather than http://.
- A padlock icon appears at the right-hand end of the Status Bar (see Figure 9-1, 163).
- Double-click the padlock to see the site's security *certificate*. The address should match the site you are viewing.
- Internet Explorer displays another warning box when you leave the secure server.

IS IT SAFE TO USE MY CREDIT CARD ONLINE?

Generally speaking, yes. In fact you are safer using a credit card than using a debit card or bank draft. Credit card companies generally provide some form of fraud protection and limits on theft. With a debit card, someone could wipe out your entire account.

Remember; only use a secure server when purchasing items using a credit card. Otherwise you risk having your information stolen.

Also, never respond to e-mails that request credit card information. Phishers routinely use e-mails to steal personal and financial information from unsuspecting recipients.

Some of these phishing e-mails may even seem to originate from your financial institution. If you ever receive an e-mail from your bank or credit card company asking for information, do not respond, but instead, call customer service.

WHAT IS EBAY?

eBay is an Internet community of buyers and sellers. People from all over the globe use eBay to buy and sell merchandise and services. Some people even earn a nice living as an eBay seller.

eBay started as a simple Internet auction site. However, over the years it has grown into a powerful and dynamic electronic marketplace. In fact, some businesses center around buying and selling on eBay.

As an Internet commerce site, most transactions occur electronically and over the Internet. Buyers can pay sellers with checks or other traditional methods. However, more often than not, money changes hand electronically by credit cards.

Being an eBay shopper means you have a near-ly unlimited choice of items to purchase. As an eBay seller you can place almost any item for sale with minimal setup costs.

IS EBAY SAFE?

eBay is very safe if you use common sense. Thousands of transactions occur daily without incident. Here's a few tips to help keep you safe on eBay:

- Always check the seller's feedback rating.
- Use *PayPal* whenever you can.
- Have your items shipped with a carrier that offers a tracking service.
- Never give bank account or credit card information to the seller.
- Avoid buying high-value antiques.
- Don't hesitate to ask the seller questions about the auction.
- Always read, then re-read, the item description.

WHAT CAN I BUY ON EBAY?

You can buy virtually anything imaginable on eBay. Here's a short list of some of the item categories on eBay:

- Housewares — dishes, curtains, and kitchen appliances
- Collectibles (dolls, coins, etc)
- Computer hardware and software
- Cars, boats, planes
- Real Estate — time shares, vacation rentals, or primary residencies
- Plants and seeds
- Professional services
- Toys and games
- Tools and building supplies
- Furniture
- Clothes and costumes

For a complete book on eBay, check out *The Senior's Guide to eBay*.

WHAT IS PAYPAL?

PayPal is an online credit card service owned by eBay. Before PayPal, sellers had to set up special merchant accounts with financial institutions such as banks to accept credit cards. Now, a PayPal account can allow sellers to accept a wide variety of credit cards with minimal setup fees or hassles.

PayPal also has benefits for the buyer as well. Paying with a credit card via PayPal is very secure and very fast. As a buyer you do not have to worry about the safety of the online transaction and as a seller you receive your payment almost immediately.

Lastly, because eBay owns PayPal, the service is integrated into eBay's auction system. eBay's easy to use Checkout feature can accept almost any form of payment to complete a transaction. You will probably find PayPal the most convenient and safest method to use.

Go to www.paypal.com for more information on opening an account.

Amazon is one of the Web's largest online shopping sites. Amazon sells books, music, and a lot of other stuff.

Most people go to Amazon first when looking for items. You can use Amazon to judge prices. If you find a price cheaper than Amazon's (or even eBay), it is probably a good deal.

Shopping on Amazon is very safe and reliable. Your account information is well protected and items are shipped on time.

You might give Amazon a try if you are new to online shopping. Just type www.amazon.com in your browser's Address Bar.

WHAT ABOUT SALES TAX?

Some Internet sales are subject to sales tax, and even when a site doesn't collect sales tax, consumers are technically responsible for remitting any unpaid sales tax on online purchases directly to their State.

When consumers are required to pay tax directly to the State, it is referred to as "use" tax. The only difference between sales and use tax is which person—the seller or the buyer—pays the State.

Because collecting use tax on smaller purchases is so much trouble, States have traditionally attempted to collect a use tax only on big-ticket items that require licenses, such as cars and boats.

One day though, sales tax will probably be collected by all online merchants and remitted to the appropriate state. After all, have you ever heard of a government that really wants to collect less revenue?

WHAT ABOUT SHIPPING?

When you buy something on the Web you usually have it shipped to your door. Most companies charge for the delivery.

Always read the online store's shipping policy. Look for sites that specify a "ships within" time. This shows the store has a good customer focus.

If you have the option, always choose a carrier with package tracking. This lets you follow your package from the online store to your house. By doing so, you know when the items ship.

Also, most carriers will only ship to a street address or apartment. Only the US Postal Service delivers to Post Office Boxes.

HOW DO I TRACK A PACKAGE?

Be sure to print out a copy of your order. Most companies e-mail you a confirmation of your order and a shipping tracking number.

All major carriers (UPS, FedEx, Airborne, etc.) offer some form of package tracking. To track your package, just go to the carrier's Website and look for a "Track Package" link.

You can also call the carrier to track your package. Just have your tracking number handy.

WHAT ABOUT RETURNS?

A reputable online store posts its return policy on its Website. You can usually find it under the heading of Customer Service, FAQ, Help, or Returns. We all know that we should read the small print. It really can, and does, matter.

You might want to print out the returns policy during your visit, if you anticipate you might ever have to return an item.

To make a return, you usually have to e-mail or phone the store, telling them your order number and the complete product name.

Then you have to specify your reason for wanting to return the product, along with your name, day-time phone, and e-mail and shipping addresses.

You must get their OK for the return, and that usually means they will send you something like a Return Merchandise Authorization (RMA) with a special number. You place that RMA and number in the original package with the product and send it to the special address they give you. To make sure your return does not get lost, use a service that allows order tracking, such as FedEx or UPS, or the Post Office's Priority or Express Mail.

PART 6

Travel and Finance

Travel and finance are two large areas on the Internet.

The Internet continues to drive change in the travel-reservation business. For customers, it often means cheaper airfares, more travel options and the ability to book a vacation while you finish a midnight snack.

Online investing has evolved along with the WWW. The emergence of discount brokers combined with the popularity of the Internet as a credible and seemingly bottomless source of investment information has given rise to do-it-yourself investing. The potential cost savings and practicality of the Web make it easy to get started.

CAN I BUY AIRLINE TICKETS ONLINE?

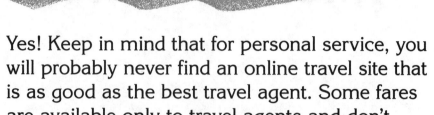

Yes! Keep in mind that for personal service, you will probably never find an online travel site that is as good as the best travel agent. Some fares are available only to travel agents and don't appear on any of the Web sites. However, many airlines post special deals that are only available on their Web site so it's worth checking directly.

When buying tickets online, keep these tips in mind:

- Check several of the online travel sites to see what flights are available and at what price.
- After you have found a likely airline, check that airline's site to see if they have any special deals.
- Check flights and prices that service nearby airports. Sometimes you can get a big savings by using a different airport.
- Compare online prices with a travel agent to see if they can beat your price.
- Most tickets are e-tickets. You just show up with an I.D. and a confirmation number and the check-in agent will then issue you a boarding pass.

CAN I RESERVE A HOTEL ROOM ONLINE?

Yes! Almost all of the online travel sites have a place where you can make a hotel reservation. Often you can purchase combination packages that can save you money on plane tickets, hotel rooms, and automobile rentals.

Or, if you have a favorite hotel, you can book a room directly with them. Just go directly to their site and type in your destination and travel dates. You can find room availability, pricing, amenities, distance to local attractions and so much more.

HOW CAN I FIND TRAVEL DEALS?

You can find the best travel deals online using discount fare-based sites such as PriceLine and Travelocity.

These sites work by letting you place bids on unsold seats on airlines. You must have a flexible travel schedule though. If you want to get somewhere and have a flexible travel schedule, then consider one of these sites. But be warned, on some of these sites if you put in a request, you have agreed to purchase that seat.

Some travel sites have a fare watcher feature. You enter your destination and it e-mails you, on a certain schedule or price point, the airfare.

HOW CAN I ACCESS MY BANK ACCOUNT ONLINE?

Your bank must offer online banking before you can access your account. Most banks do offer some form of Internet banking. Check with your bank for more information.

If they do, you can check your balances, pay loans, pay bills, transfer money, and much more. Some institutions let you download transactions in Quicken or Money file formats to make records-keeping easier.

When you access your account, be sure you are using a secure (https) connection. **Also don't share your username and password with anyone.**

HOW CAN I INVEST ONLINE?

You can have an online brokerage account that allows you to buy and sell stocks and bonds directly without help from a broker. Because you are not asking for advice, online brokerage services can lower the fees you pay to buy and sell stocks, bonds, etc.

Also, to invest online you should get a broad-band Internet connection. The reliability and speed of these connections ensure that your transactions complete.

WHERE CAN I OPEN AN INVESTMENT ACCOUNT?

There are plenty of online brokerages trading over the Internet; Fidelity, Schwab, AmeriTrade, and ScottTrade just to name a few.

However, choosing a broker requires some forethought on your part. Before picking a broker you should consider the following:

- How much do I have to invest, $500 or $500,000. Some brokers have minimum investment amounts.
- What type of investing will you do? Are you interested in stocks, bonds, mutual funds, etc? Some brokers provide better stock trading services and limited mutual fund choices.
- Consider the commission fee and schedule. If you are an active trader you probably want a site with low commission rates.

IS INVESTING ONLINE SAFE?

Yes, people and companies complete billions of dollars in investment transactions everyday over the Internet. Just like online shopping, common sense rules apply.

Here are a few tips to help you invest safely online:

- Ensure you use a secure connection. The URL prefix should be https:// and a padlock should appear in the lower right corner of the browser.
- Make sure you have your broker's phone number. The Internet, computers, and servers do break. If you need to make a trade you can always call your broker.
- Only open accounts with reputable, established brokerage houses.
- Always check your brokerage account statements for any anomalies.
- Never give out the username, password, or account numbers of your brokerage account in an e-mail or on any other Web site that is not your broker's.

HOW DO I CHECK FOR STOCK QUOTES?

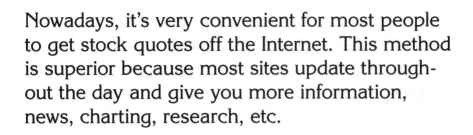

Nowadays, it's very convenient for most people to get stock quotes off the Internet. This method is superior because most sites update throughout the day and give you more information, news, charting, research, etc.

To get quotes, simply enter the ticker symbol into the quote box of any major financial site like Yahoo! Finance, CBS Marketwatch, or Quicken.com. You interpret the quotes exactly as you would with the newspaper.

Be aware that most quotes are delayed, usually by about twenty minutes. You can get real-time quotes if you have an active broker account or subscribe to an Internet-based financial service.

WHAT IS YAHOO! FINANCE?

Yahoo! Finance is probably the most popular Web site that provides the full spectrum of financial services and information. Check it out at <u>finance.yahoo.com</u>.

The site provides plenty of information on:

- Mutual funds — get current information on all types of mutual funds including returns and safety.
- Insurance — get quotes for life, home, and auto insurance.
- Interest rates — track interest rates to determine if you want to refinance your mortgage.
- Financial news — read breaking news and top stories about companies as well as earnings.
- Taxes — the latest on the IRS tax code and links to tax forms.
- Autos — provides book values on new and used cars.

PART 7

E-mail

Along with the WWW, e-mail is one of the most used aspects of the Internet. Corporations rely on e-mail as a major resource in conducting business. Individuals use e-mail extensively to keep in touch with friends and family.

In this Part we introduce you to electronic mail, or e-mail. It will step you through process of setting up an account and sending and receiving e-mail.

WHAT IS E-MAIL?

E-mail is short for electronic mail. It is digital correspondence that is fast, easy, and inexpensive.

E-mail gives you the ability to send and receive messages to and from anyone with an e-mail address. You can attach files, pictures, or programs to your message.

E-mail provides almost near instant communications. It is a very speedy way to get a message to someone. Depending upon your connection speed, someone can receive an e-mail within seconds or minutes.

E-mail is more like a conversation than a formal correspondence. It should be concise and to the point, as well as, well written. Do not forget to check your spelling, grammar and punctuation. Your teachers were right, spelling counts!

WHAT DO I NEED TO START E-MAILING?

Before starting to e-mail, you need to be able to go online using your modem, DSL, cable modem or a satellite dish.

You must have an account with an ISP, and an e-mail provider. More than likely your ISP will be your e-mail provider as well.

You will also need to have an e-mail software program, called a client. You may use a stand-alone application or use a Web browser. Netscape Navigator has an e-mail client built into it. Some e-mail providers let you access your e-mail on a Web page.

You have to have an e-mail address. Your e-mail provider will give you this.

Setting up your e-mail client is simple. The exact steps you follow to send and receive mail, will vary from program to program. However, the e-mail options are always prominently displayed on the Menu screen and in their own drop-down menus.

WHAT IS AN E-MAIL CLIENT?

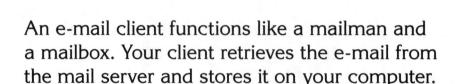

An e-mail client functions like a mailman and a mailbox. Your client retrieves the e-mail from the mail server and stores it on your computer.

Your client retrieves e-mail from the mail server using one of following two methods:

- Post Office Protocol version 3 (POP3) — basic receive protocol used between your client and the server.
- Internet Mail Access Protocol (IMAP) — an advanced protocol in which the client has more control over the server.

The e-mail server dictates the protocol you will use. More advanced servers use IMAP and provide features like multiple mail folders and search capabilities.

WHAT IS WEBMAIL?

Webmail is when you use your browser as an e-mail client. Some mail systems have Web pages that can access their e-mail systems.

This allows you to check your e-mail from any-where in which you have Internet access, wheth-er you use your own computer, or someone else's. So if you use a public computer, you can still send and receive e-mail. Or if you go on vacation you can check your e-mail just by navi-gating to the Webmail site.

One disadvantage of Webmail is that the Webpage may not provide many features. You may not have access to spell checkers or an ad-dress book. Also some Webmail clients make it difficult to attach files.

However, if your e-mail provider has a Webmail site, learn how to use it because you never know when you'll need it. AOL, MSN, and other "big" name e-mail providers all have Webmail sites.

WHAT IS SMTP?

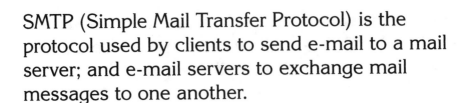

SMTP (Simple Mail Transfer Protocol) is the protocol used by clients to send e-mail to a mail server; and e-mail servers to exchange mail messages to one another.

Just as TCP and HTTP are the backbone of the Internet and WWW respectively, SMTP is the backbone of e-mail.

On your computer, the client sends e-mail to the server using SMTP. Remember it uses POP or IMAP to retrieve it.

E-mail servers then relay the e-mail to other e-mail servers using SMTP.

What does this mean to you? Some day you may want to "look under the hood", to set-up an e-mail account. Knowing a little about the protocols can make the process easier.

HOW DO I CHOOSE AN E-MAIL PROGRAM?

Most mail programs let you compose messages in a word-processor type window, send messages, check your mail box for incoming mail, read and file messages you receive, and store the e-mail addresses of people you correspond with.

Choose a mail program that complements your style of work.

The most popular programs are:

- Outlook Express — Microsoft's free e-mail program. Outlook Express is bundled with Microsoft's Web Browser, Internet Explorer.
- Outlook — Microsoft's commercial e-mail product included with Microsoft Office.
- Eudora — This free e-mail program runs under Windows and Macintosh computers.
- Netscape — The Netscape browser includes an e-mail program called Netscape Mail.

WHAT'S IN AN E-MAIL ADDRESS?

Your e-mail provider assigns an e-mail address to you. Normally you can choose your user name.

Here is an example of an address:

rscolmer@theseniorsguide.com

The first part of the address (before the @) is the user name. The second part, or domain name, defines the Internet provider where the mail is sent. The two parts are separated by an @ sign (pronounced "at").

The domain name is followed by an extension that indicates the type of organization to which the network belongs.

The complete e-mail address is unique, just like your street address.

HOW DO I SEND E-MAIL?

All e-mail clients vary so the exact method depends upon your software. Nonetheless, here's the general method to send an e-mail:

1. Start your e-mail program.
2. Click on the **Compose New Message** button. Depending on your e-mail program, the button name may vary.
3. In the To box, type the address of the recipient or click on a name in the Address Book. You can specify one or more recipients.
4. Type a short description of your e-mail on the Subject line.
5. Click anywhere in the message area and type your message.
6. To send the message, click the **Send** button.

Most people with dial-up connections compose all of their e-mail messages offline. This saves connection time that you buy from your ISP. Before you can actually send the message, you need to go online.

HOW DO I RECEIVE AND READ E-MAIL?

To check for new e-mail:

1. Be online if you have a dial-up connection.
2. Start your e-mail program.
3. Check for new messages. When new mail arrives, you will hear a sound, get a message and/or see a little envelope icon in your system tray.
4. Your mail program collects all the messages on your mail server and displays them in your InBox.
5. Double-click the new message to read it.

Most people with dial-up connections read all of their mail offline to save connection time.

Once you have read a message, your e-mail program will give you choices for handling the message. You can read and close the message, or you can choose to print the message. You can also reply to the sender, everyone, or forward it to someone else. Or you can delete the message.

WHAT IS AN E-MAIL ATTACHMENT?

Any file linked to an e-mail message is an attachment. Many mail packages use MIME (Multipurpose Internet Mail Extensions) encoding to attach files. This allows users to exchange files/documents through e-mail.

Using attachments provides an easy way for people to share documents. We co-author the Senior's Guide series using e-mail and attachments.

However, attachments are also a major source of viruses. Be sure to use anti-virus software that scans e-mail attachments. **Also, never open an attachment from strangers.**

HOW DO I OPEN AN ATTACHMENT?

When someone sends you an e-mail with an attachment, you will generally see it as an icon at the bottom of your e-mail, with its name next to it. In most cases, you can double-click the icon to open it.

Do not open an attachment if you do not know who sent it to you. Some attachments can contain viruses that can harm your hard disk or steal personal information. Even if you know the sender, make sure you do a virus scan on the attachment.

As an example, a friend recently received an e-mail from an acquaintance. The e-mail included a greeting card titled "Happy05.exe". When he opened it, it was a fireworks animation. Very pretty, but it was a virus. This particular virus hid in his computer and sent itself to people on his e-mail list without his knowledge.

This particular virus was an e-mail *worm* and was a nuisance rather than being malicious. We want to point out that you can receive a virus even from a known source of e-mail.

Once again, an anti-virus program with an automatic e-mail checker is a great tool.

HOW DO I DELETE AN E-MAIL?

Remember, each e-mail program treats e-mails slightly differently. However, this is the general method:

1. Click once to highlight the e-mail message line in your Inbox. You don't even have to open a message to delete it.
2. Press the Delete key on the keyboard. Some programs have a Delete icon on the tool bar that you can use instead.
3. Right mouse click on the Trash Can icon and choose Empty Trash to permanently delete the e-mail.

One important note to remember, when you delete the message, most mail programs put the deleted message in a "Trash" folder. Until you empty the trash, the message remains on your system.

HOW DO I REPLY TO A MESSAGE?

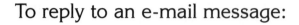

To reply to an e-mail message:

1. Click on the e-mail to open it.
2. Click on the **Reply** button. This will automatically copy the original message and address it back to the sender.
3. Type your reply message.
4. Click the **Send** button.

HOW DO I FORWARD E-MAIL?

To forward an e-mail:

1. Click the **Forward** button.
2. In the To Box, type the address of the person you want to forward mail to.
3. Click the **Send** button.

HOW DO I SEND AN ATTACHMENT?

To send a file, such as a word processing document, spreadsheet, or an image:

1. Start composing your e-mail as normal.
2. Look in the mail menu for Attach File or Send Attachments. Or, look for a "paper clip" icon on the toolbar. Click on it.
3. A dialog box will open and you will be prompted for the file name you want to attach and its location on your hard drive. You can use the Browse button to find your file if you cannot remember the path name.
4. Once you navigate to the file, double-click on it. A copy of it will be attached to your e-mail. When you actually send your e-mail, the attached file will be sent right along with it.

WHAT IS SPAM?

Spam is unsolicited "junk" e-mail sent to large numbers of people to promote products or services. Spam also refers to inappropriate promotional or commercial postings to discussion groups or bulletin boards.

Once you start e-mailing consistently you will start receiving spam. It's an unfortunate fact about the Internet.

The range of goods and services promoted in spam is endless. Here are a few examples:

- Refinancing offers
- Porn or singles Websites
- Medication such as Viagra
- Home loans
- Refurbished computers and accessories

WHAT IS AN E-MAIL WORM?

An e-mail worm is a type of virus that accesses your address book and sends itself to everyone in it. That means all your friends, relatives and business associates may get the worm as well.

Worms are dangerous and can bring e-mail servers and systems to a halt.

The best defense against a worm is anti-virus software that scans your e-mail. Without it you run the risk of getting and spreading a worm.

IS SPAM DANGEROUS?

Yes and no. Spam for the most part is dishonest, pornographic, or a scam. Nobody should have to be exposed to it, but we are.

Spam e-mail can contain viruses. As we've mentioned, it's best to use anti-virus software that has spam detection capabilities. This will significantly reduce the chance of a virus infecting your computer.

Also, some spam is from phishers looking for information.

It's best to follow the Golden Rule of Spam: Don't read or respond, just delete.

IS SPAM ILLEGAL?

This is a grey area, kind of like telemarketers. Some States have anti-spam laws and have even prosecuted spammers.

The Federal government has begun passing anti-spam laws. Although weak, the laws provide a starting point.

In the meantime, spam is something we must all live with. But the future looks better.

SHOULD I RESPOND TO SPAM?

No! Never respond to spam.

Many spam messages include a line that instructs you how to get off their e-mail lists. These remove lists rarely work. Most of the time the spammers use this as a method for verifying that your address is real so they can send you even MORE spam.

Worse yet, the e-mail may point you to a site that will secretly download a virus or Spyware onto your computer. Or it might be a phishing e-mail and try to extract personal or financial data from you.

To become better informed about spam check out www.abuse.net or www.spam.abuse.net.

Never open a spam e-mail. Never respond to a spam e-mail. The only thing to do with a suspected spam e-mail is to delete it.

WHERE CAN I GET A SPAM FILTER?

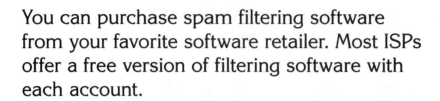

You can purchase spam filtering software from your favorite software retailer. Most ISPs offer a free version of filtering software with each account.

While spam filtering is not perfect, there are some excellent software solutions for helping with the spamming problem. Here are some things to consider before purchasing software:

- Ease of use.
- Effective at filtering.
- E-mail processing rules.
- Allow blocking of e-mails from certain people or domains.
- Block e-mail based on content categories.
- Custom rule creation for blocking e-mails.
- Quarantine area to hold infected files to keep your other files safe.

The correct use of a spam filter can once again give you, the user, complete control of your inbox.

PART 8

IM, Newsgroups and Chat Rooms

There are millions of people online and there are many ways to communicate with people and friends who share your interests. *IM (Instant Messaging)* is extremely popular these days, especially with the younger crowd. *Newsgroups*, message boards and chat rooms are also popular.

In this Part we cover how to get started using these Internet communication technologies.

WHAT IS IM?

IM is a service that enables you to create a private chat room with another person to communicate in real time on the Internet. It is similar to a telephone conversation but uses text-based, not voice-based communication.

IM provides a real-time way to chat with a friend or co-worker. You can discuss the weather, TV shows, sporting events, or anything else using IM.

Major Internet sites such as Yahoo!, America OnLine (AOL), and MSN all offer an IM service. Best of all, it's all free! They make money by enticing people to buy the "pro" service, which you really don't need.

WHAT DO I NEED TO IM?

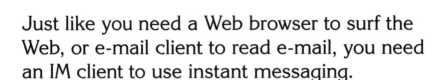

Just like you need a Web browser to surf the Web, or e-mail client to read e-mail, you need an IM client to use instant messaging.

The client you use depends on the IM provider you choose. You can choose either Yahoo! Messenger, MSN Messenger, or AOL IM. Just go to their site and sign up.

You will need to create a screen name, which is your nickname. With all the people using IM, a lot of good screen names are taken. Nonetheless, you can probably use your name plus a number without any problem.

Also, you must use a client built for your IM provider. The Yahoo! Messenger client will not communicate with the MSN IM client. So you and your friends or family need to use the same system to be able to communicate.

Needless to say, you must be connected to the Internet while you are IM'ing. Unlike, e-mail, you cannot create a message offline, then connect to send it.

HOW DO I SET UP AN AOL IM?

AOL Instant Messenger (AIM for short) is very popular and available to non-AOL subscribers. If by chance you are already using Netscape then you probably already have a copy of AIM. AIM is also packaged with a number of other software packages.

If you don't already have AIM, go to their Web site: www.aim.com. From there just follow the instructions to download it.

It will ask you to pick a screen name and password. It will also ask for your e-mail address.

After registering you can download and install the program. By default, AIM will run in the background every time you are online.

HOW DOES THE BUDDY LIST WORK?

You have to create a buddy list before you can send messages. To add a buddy:

1. Click the group to which you want to add a name.
2. Click the **Add Buddy** button.
3. Type the buddy's name and press **Enter**. (If you know the e-mail address but not the screen name, return to the AIM window and choose People. Find a Buddy Wizard. The Wizard will help you match the address to the name.)

HOW DO I SEND A BUDDY A MESSAGE?

Once you are logged in to the IM system, sending a message is easy. Here are the basic steps. Most systems work in the same manner:

To send a message to a buddy:

1. Double-click the buddy's name to open a message window.
2. Type the message.
3. Click the **Send** button.
4. AIM pops up a window on the recipient's machine. Then you and your buddy can send messages back and forth.
5. To end the conversation, just close the window.

Sending an instant message is like walking up to someone that you know, on the street, and striking up a conversation. It may or may not be convenient for them to chat with you. (Become familiar with AIM's Warn and Block feature.) Consider the following rules of etiquette:

- Unless you have a very good reason, don't send messages to people you don't know. If you must send a message, make sure it is in good taste.
- Consider the content. If it's too complicated it's probably better to send an e-mail or call them.
- Keep messages brief: no more than a sentence or two.
- Be kind. Never deliver bad news or major announcements by IM.
- Be careful. Never include sensitive or confidential information in an IM.
- Start every exchange by asking if you're interrupting. ("Is this a good time to chat?")
- Many IM programs have icons that you can set to indicate your status: Available, On The Phone, Do Not Disturb and Away. Use them.

WHAT IS A NEWSGROUP?

A newsgroup is an online discussion or forum group. It is an electronic bulletin board of messages. People from all over the world can respond to other people's messages. You can even start new discussions.

Each newsgroup is focused on a particular topic. Usenet, is a collection of over 25,000 news-groups. When you login into a newsgroup server, you are accessing some of the Usenet system.

WHAT IS A NEWSREADER?

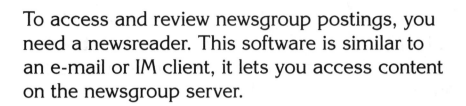

To access and review newsgroup postings, you need a newsreader. This software is similar to an e-mail or IM client, it lets you access content on the newsgroup server.

Both Microsoft Internet Explorer and Netscape Navigator come with newsreaders, but there are also freeware, shareware, and commercial stand-alone news readers.

HOW DO I ACCESS A NEWSGROUP?

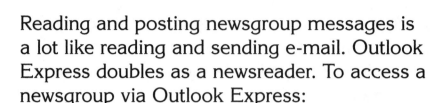

Reading and posting newsgroup messages is a lot like reading and sending e-mail. Outlook Express doubles as a newsreader. To access a newsgroup via Outlook Express:

1. Find out the address of your service provider's news server and set up Outlook Express to connect to it.
2. Start Outlook Express and go to Tools/ Accounts.
3. Click **Add/News**.
4. Enter your name and click **Next**.
5. Enter your e-mail address and click **Next**.
6. Fill in the URL of your service provider's news service.
7. When you get back to the Internet Accounts dialog box, click the News tab. You should see an entry for your news server. Select it and click the **Properties** button to give it a familiar name.
8. When you click **Close**, Outlook Express asks if you want to download newsgroups. Click **Yes**.

9. Outlook Express downloads the names of the newsgroups carried by your service provider. (Don't worry, you only have to do this once.)
10. The newsgroup list appears. Select your newsgroups and subscribe to them.
11. Click the Subscribed tab to see a list of the groups you have selected.

HOW DO I READ NEWSGROUP MESSAGES?

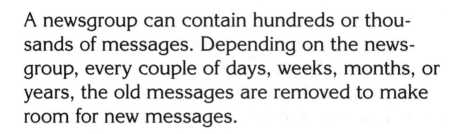

A newsgroup can contain hundreds or thousands of messages. Depending on the newsgroup, every couple of days, weeks, months, or years, the old messages are removed to make room for new messages.

You can reply to a message, which is called a follow-up. It is best to include part of the original message when you reply to a message. You can choose to reply to the author of the message or to the whole newsgroup.

You can also post a new message to a newsgroup. If you want to perform a trial run before posting a message, you can send a test message to alt.test. You will receive a reply to let you know if you posted correctly.

HOW TO FIND ARCHIVED NEWSGROUP MESSAGES?

Usenet and newsgroups have been around for over twenty years. As you might expect, a lot of messages exist. Most have been archived.

You can access an archive of all newsgroup messages using Google Groups. Google acquired DejaNews, which was the previous archiver.

To find messages at Google Groups, you enter key words in the search field. Google then searches the newsgroup archive and displays a list of messages that contain your specified keywords. To narrow your search, you can use the Power Search feature.

Check out Google Groups at groups.google.com for more information.

WHO CONTORLS A NEWGROUP?

No single group or person controls a news-group. Newsgroups are self-governing communities; there are no "Newsgroup Cops." Instead, posters regulate themselves.

Therefore keep your messages simple and professional. You never know who will read the message, so be sure to watch what you say.

Someone could forward your message to your boss, a thousand of your closest friends and clients, or post it on the front page of the *New York Times*. Remember Google archives the messages...you never know who will find your postings.

WHAT IS NEWSGROUP ETIQUETTE?

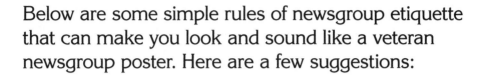

Below are some simple rules of newsgroup etiquette that can make you look and sound like a veteran newsgroup poster. Here are a few suggestions:

- Lurk — Read the newsgroup without posting for a few weeks.
- Read the Newsgroup FAQ — The FAQ (Frequently Asked Questions) can answer questions you didn't even know you had.
- Stay on-topic.
- DON'T SHOUT — ALL CAPS IS SHOUTING.
- Don't advertise — Be very hesitant about posting advertisements or commercial messages.
- Ignore "trolls" — Some people get a thrill from posting "flames" (really obnoxious messages) just to get a rise out of people. Sad, isn't it?
- Don't "spam" — Spam is posting the same message to dozens, even hundreds or thousands of unrelated newsgroups.
- Be original — Don't over-quote: Copying a long post (more than 20 lines) just to add "I agree" or "me too" is considered bad form.
- The Golden Rule — Do unto others as you would have them do unto you. Remember, every expert was a newbie once.

WHAT ARE CHAT ROOMS?

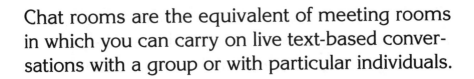

Chat rooms are the equivalent of meeting rooms in which you can carry on live text-based conversations with a group or with particular individuals.

Chats take place in a chat room, a forum, or via an Internet Relay Channel (IRC). There are two basic kinds of chats: Web based and IRC. Most Web based chat rooms are easier to access and are devoted to general subject matter.

Do you remember your mother telling you not to talk to strangers? Well, unless you already know the people in a chat room, they are all strangers. Be careful. Be smart about the information you exchange.

WHAT IS IRC?

IRC is short for Internet Relay Chat. It is very popular because it enables people connected anywhere on the Internet to join in live discussions.

To join an IRC discussion, you need an IRC client and Internet access. The IRC client is a program that runs on your computer and sends and receives messages to and from an IRC server. The IRC server is responsible for making sure that all messages are broadcast to everyone participating in the discussion.

Do a Google search on "IRC clients" to find a client. Here are a couple free ones you might consider:

- mIRC — www.mirc.com
- ircle — www.ircle.com (MacIntosh)

WHAT ARE VOICE AND VIDEO CHAT
AND WEB-BASED CHAT?

With voice and video chat, you can hear and see the person(s) you are chatting with. Your computer will need a sound card, speakers and a microphone. If you want to be seen while you chat, you will need to connect a video camera to your computer. You will also need some special software.

Web based chat (like MSN, Yahoo, and most of the "sponsored" chats) use chat software they provide on the Web site.

It's usually Java based, easy to learn, and fairly user-friendly. Web based chats have more limited features than IRC clients on your computer.

PART 9

Internet Security Basics

The openness and richness of the Internet also has its drawbacks. There are people on the Internet that will try to scam you out of money, steal your identity, or crash your computer.

In this Part we discuss security issues of the Internet and provide some hints on how to keep your personal information and computer safe. In a nutshell though, surfing safely on the Internet is a matter of common sense.

CAN I NAVIGATE THE INTERNET SAFELY?

It depends. Used correctly and intelligently the Internet is as safe as going to the mall. Used without caution or carelessly, the Internet has some dangerous aspects.

Many different dangers exist on the Internet. The types of dangers can be categorized into the following:

- Identity theft
- Phishing
- Viruses
- Spyware

Identity theft and phishing do not involve your computer except that the thieves "look at" your computer and steal personal and financial information such as your SSN or credit card numbers.

On the other hand, viruses and Spyware affect your computer. Malicious software is loaded onto your computer without your knowledge or permission. Viruses and Spyware can also be used in identity theft and phishing.

WHAT CAN HAPPEN TO MY COMPUTER?

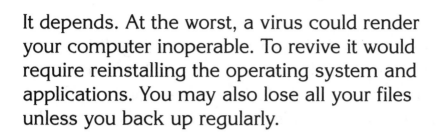

It depends. At the worst, a virus could render your computer inoperable. To revive it would require reinstalling the operating system and applications. You may also lose all your files unless you back up regularly.

A more likely scenario is that a hacker might hijack your computer and use it to attack other computers on the Internet, track your Web usage or steal personal information.

Keeping your computer up to date with security patches and using anti-virus software can reduce your chances of getting a virus.

This is fairly easy to do and does not cost a lot of money or take a lot of time. Just think of it as good housekeeping.

WHAT CAN HAPPEN TO MY PERSONAL INFORMATION?

Under normal circumstances nothing. It is virtually impossible for your personal information to just leak out into Cyberspace. Someone has to have malicious intent and the tools to "break into" your computer. Under normal usage, with a little housekeeping time, you and your computer are safe.

However, if your computer becomes infected with certain types of viruses or Spyware, then someone may be able to steal important information.

Viruses exist that can read your files and send the information to another computer, but these are extremely rare. Most of the time Spyware is installed that will read your keystrokes as you type them into a Web form or intercept data transmissions.

Using an anti-virus software, anti-spyware program, anti-ad program and a *firewall* can help protect your files to a great degree.

WHAT IS A HACKER?

Hacker is a slang term for a computer enthusiast. Among professional programmers, the term hacker implies an amateur or a programmer who lacks formal training. Depending on how it is used, the term can be either complimentary or derogatory, although it is developing an increasingly derogatory connotation.

The pejorative sense of hacker is becoming more prominent largely because the press has co-opted the term to refer to individuals who gain unauthorized access to computer systems for the purpose of stealing and corrupting data. Hackers, themselves, maintain that the proper term for such individuals is cracker.

HOW CAN I SAFELY USE THE INTERNET?

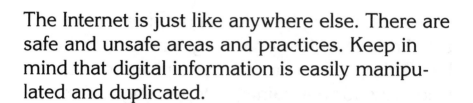

The Internet is just like anywhere else. There are safe and unsafe areas and practices. Keep in mind that digital information is easily manipulated and duplicated.

Always make sure your transactions are done over a secure server. A secure server encrypts your information. That means the information has been scrambled by software to make it unreadable by anyone but the receiving computer.

Most Web browsers include security features that let you know when your connection is secure and when it is not. A secure site is denoted with a locked padlock in the bottom bar of the browser window and the https:// prefix in the URL. Figure 9-1 on the next page shows an example of the padlock in Internet Explorer.

Another simple but important rule is to never give out your username and password to anyone over the Internet. This includes e-mail and instant messaging as well as logins to financial sites. You never know who might be watching.

FIGURE 9-1: Example of Secure Connection Using IE

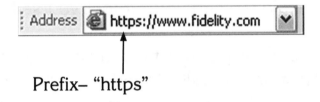

Prefix– "https"

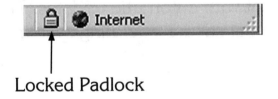

Locked Padlock

HOW DO I PROTECT MYSELF?

Security software provides reasonable protection against viruses and Spyware. It never hurts to use it. Nonetheless, education and skepticism are the best defense against identity theft and phishing. Only by learning about the ways you can be exploited can you protect yourself.

You can buy very sophisticated security software. Most are actually "bundles" consisting of software for anti-virus, spyware, firewall, anti-phishing, and anti-spam. Major vendors include TrendMicro, McAfee and Symantec.

If you run Windows you need to keep your computer current with automatic updates. This ensures the most secure operating system possible.

HOW DO I ENABLE AUTOMATIC UPDATES?

Enabling automatic updates on Windows is easy. Follow these steps to enable it on your Windows computer:

1. Click **Start** ⇨ Settings ⇨ Control Panel to open the Windows Control Panel.
2. Click on the icon named "Automatic Updates" to open the window shown in Figure 9-2.
3. Click the checkbox labeled "Keep my computer up to date."
4. Next, choose a setting that controls how the update occurs. You can choose one of three different methods that range from automatic to manual. For most people, completely automatic works best.
5. Click the **OK** or **Apply** to save your settings.

Remember, if you set a specific time of day for your computer to update itself, your computer must be on during that time frame.

Figure 9-2: Windows Automatic Update Settings

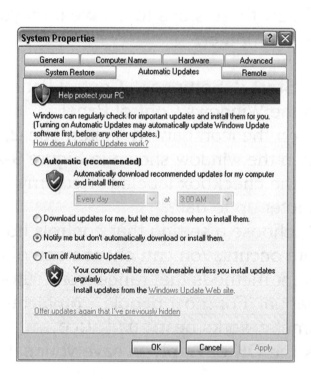

WHAT IS A COOKIE?

A *cookie* is information from a Web site stored on your hard drive that it can retrieve later. It is like an enhanced ID card that remembers your preferences. The next time you visit the site, it reads the cookie and loads any preferences you have.

Browsers let you control how Web sites use cookies. You can choose to avoid cookies all together or let Web sites use them freely. Unfortunately some sites require cookies. If you need to go to that site, you have to accept their cookie.

Cookies do provide a useful function. Most Web sites routinely log your visit and store your preferences in a cookie. These cookies contain information that is recorded against your IP address. When you revisit the site, the Web site can read the cookie and set your preferences accordingly.

For example, Google uses cookies to remember your language settings. Some sites use cookies to store your usernames or the type of news you want displayed.

ARE COOKIES DANGEROUS?

Much more often than not cookies are very safe. Cookies can be dangerous as they essentially track your computer usage. Viruses exist that can read your cookies and steal your login information.

If you use a public computer, such as at the library, you want to be extra careful. Cookies with your personal information may be stored on that computer.

If you use a public computer, it's best to delete the cookies after every use.

HOW DO I DELETE COOKIES?

With IE, deleting cookies is easy. Refer to Figure 9-3 on the next page as you follow these steps:

1. Click Tools ⇨ Internet options.
2. Click the **Delete Cookies** button under the Temporary Internet Files section located in the middle of the dialog box. This will remove all cookies.
3. Click the **OK** button to close the dialog box.

You should routinely delete cookies from your computer as part of your good housekeeping practices.

FIGURE 9-3: Deleting Cookies In IE

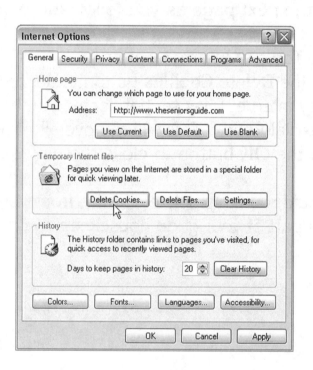

CAN I CONTROL HOW COOKIES ARE PLACED ON MY COMPUTER?

All major browsers let you control how your computer handles cookies.

You can choose almost any degree of cookie management; from no cookies allowed to all cookies allowed. To manage cookies in Internet Explorer:

1. Click the Tools ⇨ Internet Options to open the dialog box shown in Figure 9-4.
2. Click the Privacy Tab.
3. Adjust the Slider Bar to the level of security that you want.

IE uses a default setting of "Medium." This allows certain types of cookies and blocks others. Unless you understand a lot about cookies, its best to use the "Medium" or "Medium-High" setting.

FIGURE 9-4: Cookie Privacy Settings in IE

ARE THERE DIFFERENT TYPES
OF COOKIES?

Yes, two types of cookies exist. You can control how your browser handles each type.

One type of cookie is called a First-Party cookie. These are from the Web site you are currently viewing. First-Party cookies usually contain preference and user information. Web sites use first party cookies to customize their site to your browsing habits. Google uses First-Party cookies.

The other type of cookie is a called a Third-Party cookie. These cookies are from Web sites that you are not currently viewing. Pop-up ads and usage tracking Web sites utilize Third-Party cookies.

WHAT IS A FIREWALL?

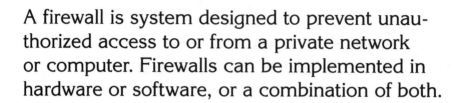

A firewall is system designed to prevent unauthorized access to or from a private network or computer. Firewalls can be implemented in hardware or software, or a combination of both.

Most home computers use a software firewall. These applications run in the background and filter network traffic coming in and going out of your computer. Blocking inbound traffic prevents hackers from accessing your computer. Blocking outbound traffic helps prevent *Trojans* from using your computer to access other computers.

Even if you have anti-virus software you should consider using a firewall. This ensures that nothing can get in or out of your computer without your knowledge.

WHERE CAN I GET A FIREWALL?

If you run Windows XP Service Pack 2 you already have a firewall installed and running. Microsoft turns on this feature by default. You can still install and use a third-party firewall if you wish.

If you run an older version of Windows, you will need to get a firewall. On a Macintosh, Mac OS X comes with a built-in firewall, it just needs to be turned on in the System Preferences. Most anti-virus software packages have firewalls included. Here's a list of the major vendors that you should consider:

- Symantec
- McAfee
- ZoneLabs
- TrendMicro

ARE WIRELESS NETWORKS SAFE?

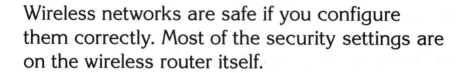

Wireless networks are safe if you configure them correctly. Most of the security settings are on the wireless router itself.

Configuring a wireless network is beyond the scope of this book. However, for the inquisitive reader, it involves configuring the following on your wireless router:

- Enabling *Wireless Encryption Protocol* (WEP). This will prevent others from viewing your wireless data.
- Specifying the MAC address of the wireless clients you want to connect to your wireless network.

If you have a friend or relative knowledgeable in computers you can have them configure these settings. Check your router's owner's manual for more details.

As a word of warning, don't operate a wireless network without setting at least one of the two items listed above.

WHAT IS A SECURE SITE?

A secure Web site is one that uses an encrypted protocol and one whose identity is well known.

The encrypted protocol used is called *SSL* (Secure Sockets Layer). When the URL starts with https://, then SSL is being used.

Verifying the identity of a Web site is done with certificates, which function as an electronic ID for a site.

Fortunately, a browser automatically switches to a secure mode when it points to a secure site. If you see a small lock in the lower right corner of the browser, you are operating in a secure mode.

WHAT ARE CERTIFICATES?

Certificates are a Web site's ID card or finger-print. They allow your browser to verify the identity of a Web site and communicate with it using SSL. Certificates help protect you from unsafe Web sites and software.

The following two types of certificates exist:

- Personal — used by individuals to identify themselves to others.
- Web site — used by a Web site to verify that it is secure and authentic. Most e-commerce sites use Web site certificates.

A certificate authority (CA) creates both personal and Web site certificates. This entity, usually a for profit company such as Equifax, verifies the identity of the certificate holder. You can safely accept certificates published by CA's.

SHOULD I ACCEPT CERTIFICATES?

You should accept certificates from entities that you trust such as Microsoft. Whenever you access a secure site using https:// you automatically download the sites certificate and Internet Explorer displays a "lock" icon in the lower right corner.

Figure 9-5 shows the dialog box that appears when you access a secure site that uses a certificate that is not published by a certificate authority.

It is your decision whether or not to accept the certificate. If you know the site is reputable, like your church or library, then it is probably safe to accept it. Otherwise don't — especially if it involves personal or financial data.

Figure 9-5 Certificate Dialog Box

PART 10

Identity Theft, Phishing, Viruses, and Spyware

Identity theft, phishing, viruses, and Spyware represent the largest security threat on the Internet. In this Part we describe each one and provide information on how to protect yourself.

WHAT IS IDENTITY THEFT?

Identity theft occurs when someone steals your personal information and pretends to be you in order to steal money or other assets from you.

Information at risk includes:

- Social Security Number
- Internet usernames and passwords
- Credit card numbers
- Bank account numbers
- And everything else you would not want a stranger to know

Identity theft is becoming a big problem on the Internet. It is hard to tell who and what to trust. With some education though, you can adequately protect yourself and use the Internet with little worry.

HOW DOES IDENTITY THEFT HAPPEN ON THE INTERNET?

Identify theft can happen many different ways on the Internet. Usually it occurs when Spyware unknowingly is loaded onto your computer.

Spyware is software that tracks your online activity such as e-mails, instant messaging, sites you visit, and downloads. This can be extremely dangerous if you access your financial information online.

Here are some examples of how a Spyware infestation can occur:

- You open a spam e-mail or any e-mail that has not been scanned by an anti-virus program. The e-mail happens to contain hidden Spyware.
- A popup ad asks you to download a required application. It tells you that it's necessary to download the application before proceeding to view the site. The download might be Spyware.
- You download a screensaver or a file from the Web and after you install it, Spyware is installed in the background without your permission.

HOW CAN I PROTECT MY IDENTITY?

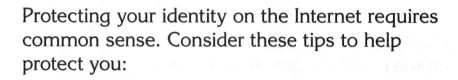

Protecting your identity on the Internet requires common sense. Consider these tips to help protect you:

- Never send credit card or personal information via e-mail. E-mails are easily intercepted.
- Use a credit card instead of a debit card for Internet purchases. This allows you to dispute a charge if needed.
- Never give out Internet passwords and change your passwords often.
- Always shop on Web sites you know and trust.
- Never answer unsolicited requests for information.
- Delete cookies often.
- Be suspicious of every incoming e-mail or ad. If an ad comes in for a product or service you really could use, go to the parent Web site by manually typing in the URL. Even then, be suspicious since they sent you a solicitation.

WHAT IS PHISHING?

Phishing (pronounced "fishing") is when someone acts as someone else with the intent of trying to extract personal information from YOU.
It is a big problem and one of the toughest to
guard against.

The main danger of being "phished" is that someone can gain access to your financial information,
passwords, Social Security number or any security information. Thieves can use the information
to make purchases or withdraw money from your
bank or investment accounts.

Phishing on the Internet typically occurs when
someone sends a misleading e-mail that asks
you to send personal information or update personal information on an imposter Web site. The
Web site is a fake and only exists to steal your information. In addition, the Web site may promise
something in return for your information.

Phishing e-mails usually contain hypertext links
that point to rouge Web sites. Do not click on any
of these links. Type the URL in the address bar
instead if you elect to go to them at all. When you
get suspicious e-mails, delete them immediately.

WHAT IS AN EXAMPLE OF PHISHING?

One of the most famous examples of phishing is the Nigerian Bank e-mail scam. The e-mail asks for your bank account number so they can move millions of dollars out of the country. Once they move the money, they promise the bank will give you a percent of the total for your effort. Needless to say these e-mails are a scam. Unfortunately, a lot of people lose money by falling for the scam.

Phishers today create more believable and sophisticated e-mails every day. As a rule ignore all e-mails with any offer. Even if you think it's from a reputable company. Skepticism pays when it comes to e-mails. Even though there is a cute name for these people, they are con artists and thieves.

HOW CAN I STOP PHISHING?

Unfortunately you cannot stop phishing. You can become educated about it and adopt some safe surfing practices.

Unlike virus software, nothing exists to completely eliminate phishing attacks. However, anti-spam software can minimize the number of phishing e-mails you receive.

Here's a list of some things you can do to minimize your chance of being phished:

- Do not click on any hypertext links in an e-mail.
- Use a pop-up blocker to keep fake pop-up browser windows from opening.
- Always type the URL in the Address Bar.
- Check your bank and credit card statements to ensure all transactions are legitimate.
- Use anti-spam software to reduce the number of nuisance and potentially fake e-mails from arriving to your inbox.
- Avoid filling out forms via e-mail.
- Delete e-mails with urgent requests for personal or financial information.

WHAT IS A VIRUS?

The term virus has come to mean any type of malicious software (i.e. malware) installed on your computer.

Strictly speaking though, a virus is any unwanted file or application that corrupts or replaces files on your computer, usually causing harm to your computer.

A virus replicates itself as the file is shared from computer to computer. Advanced viruses can self-replicate using your computer as a base station.

Viruses may infect all types of programs and files on your computer. A virus can target your operating system files or data files such as spreadsheets, word processing files or images.

DO I NEED ANTI-VIRUS SOFTWARE?

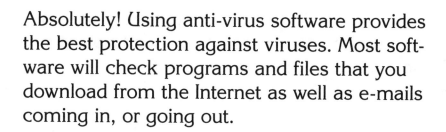

Absolutely! Using anti-virus software provides the best protection against viruses. Most software will check programs and files that you download from the Internet as well as e-mails coming in, or going out.

You're probably asking yourself why you would need to check your outgoing e-mail. After all, you know you are clean. That is part of the problem. If a virus sneaks through and you do not catch it, you can spread the virus through your outgoing e-mail.

Even people you know and trust can accidentally send you a virus so always use your virus protection program regularly.

You can purchase protection software from a computer store or the Internet. The two most popular programs are McAfee's Anti-Virus and Symantec's Norton Anti-Virus.

If your anti-virus program has an automatic update system, use it. This ensures that you always have the most current virus protection information.

HOW DOES MY COMPUTER GET A VIRUS?

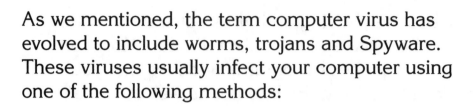

As we mentioned, the term computer virus has evolved to include worms, trojans and Spyware. These viruses usually infect your computer using one of the following methods:

- E-mail with infected attachments or embedded scripts.
- Infected files such as word processing or spreadsheets.
- Visiting malicious sites that download software to your computer.

You can adequately protect yourself by knowing where computer viruses come from. Software can only do so much, you must do the rest. Practicing safe surfing and e-mailing is the best protection of all, but only when coupled with appropriate software safeguards.

DO E-MAILS CONTAIN VIRUSES?

E-mails themselves do not specifically contain viruses. E-mail attachments can contain viruses. Also, HTML-based e-mail can include virus scripts.

Most types of attachments can contain viruses. Viruses can hide in applications, word processing files, spreadsheets, and image files. Avoid opening an attachment from an unknown source.

In addition, if you elect to open an attachment, only open an e-mail attachment after your anti-virus software has scanned it. Most anti-virus software automatically scans e-mails and attachments as you open them.

Some e-mails contain worm viruses, which read your address book then sends itself to all the entries. Therefore knowing the sender doesn't guarantee safety. Only up-to-date anti-virus software can tell if someone you know is sending you an infected e-mail. If you get a suspicious e-mail from someone, delete it without ever opening it.

HOW DO I GET RID OF A VIRUS?

To rid your computer of a virus you need anti-virus software. The software will detect and eliminate the virus.

Fortunately, you can remove most viruses from your computer. How much harm they do depends upon how long it has been on your computer and the type of virus.

Diligent use of anti-virus software can help keep most viruses off your computer.

HOW DO I CHOOSE ANTI-VIRUS SOFTWARE?

For anti-virus software, you cannot go wrong if you stick with a major vendor such as Symantec, McAfee, or TrendMicro.

Here are a few features an anti-virus package should have:

- Automated scanning of files and e-mails.
- Real-time scanning of e-mail and attachments.
- Automatic update service to download the most current virus detection information.

WHAT IS SPYWARE?

Spyware is any software that covertly gathers user information through the user's Internet connection without his or her knowledge, usually for advertising, marketing or sales purposes.

IS SPYWARE BAD?

Yes. Aside from the questions of ethics and privacy, Spyware steals from the user by using the computer's memory resources and also by eating bandwidth as it sends information back to the Spyware's home base via the user's Internet connection. Because Spyware is using memory and system resources, the applications running in the background can lead to system crashes or general system instability.

Spyware has the ability to monitor keystrokes, scan files on the hard drive, snoop other applications (such as chat programs or word processors), install other Spyware programs, read cookies, change the default home page on the Web browser, consistently relaying this information back to the Spyware author who will either use it for advertising/marketing purposes or sell the information to another party.

HOW DOES MY COMPUTER
GET SPYWARE?

Spyware applications can infect your computer
via e-mails or Web sites. Most often, a Web
site will download Spyware to your computer
without you knowing it.

Also, freeware and shareware may contain
Spyware, although the majority do not.

HOW DO I PREVENT OR REMOVE SPYWARE?

Like viruses, Spyware requires software to remove it. The prevention and removal of Spyware is now a thriving cottage industry.

Most major security vendors offer some form of Spyware removal software, usually bundled with their anti-virus software. Microsoft has a free Spyware tool that you may want to try. However, it does not provide any virus protection.

When using Spyware protection software you need to ensure that your software is up-to-date. New Spyware is being deployed everyday. Therefore it is important to keep your Spyware-removal software is up-to-date.

The three programs we use are:

- Spybot
- SpyWareBlaster
- AdAware

They are all free and easy to install.

CONCLUSION

We hope that you got excited by what you can do on, and with, the Internet. That is what Parts 1-8 were meant to do.

We included Parts 9 and 10 to remind you that just as in the real world, the Internet world requires you to "look over both shoulders" and exercise safety precautions.

We know you will have years of fun and enjoyment with these new tools. So get out there and start surfing, e-mailing and shopping!

25 TIPS FOR USING THE INTERNET

1. Know who you're dealing with. If the company is unfamiliar, check with your state or local consumer protection agency and the Better Business Bureau. Some Web sites have feedback forums, which can provide useful information about other people's experiences with particular sellers. Get the physical address and phone number in case there is a problem.

2. Look for information about how complaints are handled. It can be difficult to resolve complaints, especially if the seller or charity is located in another country. Look on the Web site for information about programs the company or organization participates in that require it to meet standards for reliability and help to handle disputes.

3. Be aware that "no complaints" is no guarantee. Fraudulent operators open and close quickly, so the fact that no one has made a complaint yet doesn't mean that the seller or charity is legitimate. You still need to look for other danger signs of fraud.

4. Don't believe promises of easy money. If someone claims that you can earn money with little or no work, get a loan or credit card even if you have bad credit, or make money with little or no risk, it's likely a scam.

5. Resist pressure. Legitimate companies and charities will be happy to give you time to make a decision. It's probably a scam if they demand that you act immediately or won't take "No" for an answer.

6. Think twice before entering contests operated by unfamiliar companies. Fraudulent marketers sometimes use contest entry forms to identify potential victims.

7. Be cautious about unsolicited e-mails. They are often fraudulent. If you are familiar with the company or charity that sent you the e-mail and you don't want to receive further messages, send a reply asking to be removed from the e-mail list. However, responding to unknown senders may simply verify that yours is a working e-mail address and result in even more unwanted messages from strangers. The best approach may simply be to delete the e-mail.

8. Beware of imposters. Someone might send you an e-mail pretending to be connected with a business or charity, or create a Web site that looks just like that of a well-known company or charitable organization. If you're not sure that you're dealing with the real thing, find another way to contact the legitimate business or charity and ask.

9. Guard your personal information. Don't provide your credit card or bank account number unless you are actually paying for something. Your social security number should not be necessary unless you are applying for credit. Be especially suspicious if someone claiming to be from a company with whom you have an account asks for information that the business already has.

10. Beware of "dangerous downloads." In download-

200

ing programs to see pictures, hear music, play games, etc., you could download a virus that wipes out your computer files or connects your modem to a foreign telephone number, resulting in expensive phone charges. Only download programs from Web sites you know and trust

11. Pay the safest way. Credit cards are the safest way to pay for online purchases because you can dispute the charges if you never get the goods or services or the offer was misrepresented. Federal law limits your liability to $50 if someone makes unauthorized charges to your account.

12. When adding images to your Web pages, you should use GIF or JPEG images. These are the most popular types of images on the Web.

13. Each Web browser will display your Web pages in a slightly different way.

14. A bounced message is a message that returns to you because it cannot reach its destination.

15. If you choose a DSL or cable Internet account, the phone company or cable company usually supplies the modem. If you choose a dial-up account you have to get our own modem.

16. Pages with large pictures or a lot of content are sometimes slow to load; sometimes the net itself is just slow. Also, when things seem to be so slow that you suspect they've stopped, your network connection may have gone down (perhaps your phone is disconnected, or your

Internet software needs to be restarted, or your Internet service provider is down).

17. Try to avoid a lot of clicking ahead; clicking over and over on a spot won't make the page load any faster, and will make it slower.

18. If you click on a link before a page has finished loading, you will interrupt the transfer of data. Then, the links going to later places within that page (like the links at the top of this page) won't all work, and the computer won't tell you why. At this point, reload the page; to do this, click on the "reload" or "refresh" button.

19. Some pages no longer exist. When this is the case, you'll usually get a message telling you that the file was not found. At this point, going back to the previous page (using the "Back" button) is the easiest option.

20. Take advantage of online banking, investing, and bill pay. It's safe and saves you time.

21. Choose a home page that gives you the information you need. Yahoo! and MSN are great choices.

22. Don't forget to empty your Trash in your e-mail client. Messages stick around until you do.

23. Choose the fastest Internet connection you can afford. Faster speeds make a difference.

24. Let virus software scan your system everyday.

25. Download large PDF files and read them. Reading them online is very slow.

GLOSSARY

applet — a small Java-based application that runs from a Web site.

ActiveX — small add-in programs, similar to plug-ins that enhances a browser's capabilities.

blog — short for "weB LOG", essentially an online diary focusing on specialized topics.

broadband — a high-speed Internet connection; includes DSL, ISDN, cable modem, or satellite.

cable modem — a device used to connect to the Internet using the cable TV line.

certificate — a digital id card that verifies the identity of a Web site, usually issued by a certificate authority.

cookie — a text file placed on your computer by a Web site and used to store information like usernames, passwords, and preferences.

dial-up connection — the most simple, slowest, and cheapest method of connecting to an ISP, using standard telephone line.

DSL (Digital Subscriber Line) — a high-speed data line provided by the telephone company; technically known as ADSL (Asynchronous Digital Subscriber Line).

eBay — the largest online auction site.

e-mail — a system built on the Internet that allows computer users to exchange messages.

firewall — a software or hardware system that blocks incoming and outgoing network data.

GLOSSARY

File Transfer Protocol (FTP) — a method of uploading and downloading.

Google — the de-facto standard search engine on the Web found at www.google.com.

Home Page — the default Web site that loads when you start your browser.

Hyper-Text Markup Language (HTML) — the programming code used to create Web pages.

Hyper-Text Transfer Protocol (HTTP) — The common "language" used between WWW servers and Web browsers.

instant messaging (IM) — typically a text-base real-time chat, usually one on one. AOL, MSN, Yahoo! all have chat systems.

Internet — an International network of servers and clients and that allows services such as e-mail, newsgroups, and the World Wide Web.

Internet Service Provider (ISP) — an entity, usually a commercial company, that provides a connection point onto the Internet.

ISDN — a special, high-speed digital telephone that provides broadband connection rates.

Internet Relay Chat (IRC) — a real-time chat system built for multiple users.

Java — a programming language by Sun Microsystems and used by Web developers.

modem — a simple device that allows computers to communicate over telephone, cable, or satellites.

GLOSSARY

MP3 files — an audio file format that most media players can play.

multimedia — use of computers to combine text, video, animation, and sound into files or Web sites.

newsgroups — a system built on the Internet that allows users to create community message boards on any topic.

PayPal — eBay's credit card processing company.

phishing — pronounced "fishing", a term used when someone tries to steal personal information by mis-representing themselves.

plug-in — auxiliary programs that enhance a browser's capability.

pop-up — a browser window that "pops up" when you navigate to some Web sites and usually contains advertisements.

QuickTime — a multimedia player from Apple that works on both Macs and PCs.

RealPlayer — a multimedia player that plays most multimedia files.

search engine — a Web-based program the searches indexed Web pages.

SMTP (Simple Mail Transfer Protocol) — The "language" used between e-mail servers to exchange email messages.

spam — junk e-mail that may contain viruses.

GLOSSARY

Spyware — a form of virus that tracks Internet usage or extracts personal information from your computer.

SSL — Secure Sockets Layer, used for secure Web browsing and indicated by https in the address bar.

TCP/IP — Transmission Control Protocol/Internet Protocol, which is the language used by computers on the Internet.

Trojan — a virus that is planted on your computer and takes control of it.

URL (Uniform Resource Locator) — an address of a Web site, e.g. www.theseniorsguide.com.

viruses — malicious software loaded unknowingly onto a computer; Spyware.

Web browser — a software application that allows you to access HTML documents on a Web server.

Webmail — an e-mail client that runs in a browser.

WebTV — a small Internet-appliance that transforms your television into an Internet device.

Wireless Encryption Protocol (WEP) — a protocol used by wireless routers to encrypt wireless network communications.

worm — an e-mail virus that propagates by sending itself to your address book contacts.

WWW — a system built on the Internet using hypertext links and provides text, images, video and sound content.

INDEX

INDEX